DEDICATION

This book is dedicated to the wonderful, loving memory of my Bible college pastor, Rev. Jonathan Urshan, who instilled a love for the gifts of the Spirit, moving of the Spirit and end time prophecy. A Persian, he was raised in Israel until he was 18. He spoke six languages fluently including Hebrew and Arabic. His knowledge of Bible places and customs and the language was native, from first hand observation. He spoke often on radio talk shows and was a frequent end time conference speaker around the world. He worked closely with Israel to help that nation realize the dream of establishing temple sacrifice. His teachings were thrilling, He was a man who loved me in such a way as I always felt that I was another son to him.

INTRODUCTION

End time prophecy is a subject many people want to know about, but few people truly understand. Control is the point, right? Tell me my future, tell me what is going to happen so I can have some control over which I have no control now. We have heard the cliché: knowledge is power and foreknown is forewarned. That is why many people seek out palm readers, psychics, etc. However, with Biblical prophecy, personal control is not the point or the goal.

The Bible says in **Ecclesiastes 7:12**:

12 For wisdom is a defence, and money is a defence: but the excellency of knowledge is, that wisdom giveth life to them that have it.

The life that is gained by wisdom though the study of prophecy is the knowledge of God's predetermined events, and the predetermined plan of escape. We will take an intense look at both in this study.

The Biblical timeline of God serves as safe steppingstones across the tumultuous rapids of world affairs and events. Man plans chaos for personal gain. God plans safety and peace out of love for His people, and deliverance from evil.

Exodus 15:3

3 The Lord is a man of war: the Lord is his name.

Before the creation of earth, God first created angels, some of which chose to rebel. Subsequently, there has been a fight, a war between good and evil. God allows this war because it perfects freedom of choice in mankind. The struggle of man amplified by deception of demons, has plagued this world since the Garden. God is still growing a garden. He wants a harvest of people that have chosen Him and refused evil by choice.

James 5:7-8

7 Be patient therefore, brethren, unto the coming of the Lord. Behold, the husbandman waiteth for the precious fruit of the earth, and hath long patience for it, until he receive the early and latter rain.

8 Be ye also patient; stablish your hearts: for the coming of the Lord draweth nigh.

As a vine dresser might have several varieties of grapes which he blends to make wine, so also, the Lord has two special vintages: the Church and the Jewish nation. When the harvest is ripe and come to the full, it will be harvested, and all else to be discarded as chaff. I want to be picked, not discarded, don't you?

To know and understand the plan of God gives a peace that cannot be comprehended outside of God. He knows what is happening, He is controlling it, and He knows how events will unfold. He knows where

I am, where I will be, and how to take care of me and my family. His intentions are to bless those that seek Him and there are rewards for both good and evil. Each accrues wages (Romans 6:23).

As you read through this study, we, Dennis and Linda, hope your questions will be answered, but more than that, our hope is that this knowledge you hold in your hand will lead you to a hunger for God and a closer relationship with Him unlike any you have experienced to this point in your life. But be forewarned, you must prepare exactly according to the dictates of His Word, and not religious traditions of men, because, David said in Psalm 119:89, "Forever, O Lord, thy word is settled in heaven." And also, Jesus in John 12:48 said, "...the word that I have spoken, the same will judge him in the last day." Considering the events of prophecy and warnings of scripture, it would behoove us to diligently seek out the Book of God and see what things are so. We concur with Martin Luther and John Wesley:

"Since your Majesty and your Lordships desire a simple reply, I will answer without horns and without teeth. Unless I am convicted by scripture and plain reason – I do not accept the authority of popes and counsels, for they have contradicted each other – my conscious is captive to the word of God. I cannot and I will not recant anything, for to go against conscious is neither right nor safe. God help me, here I stand. I cannot do otherwise." Martin Luther, 1521

"I want to know one thing, the way to heaven; how to land safe on that happy shore. God Himself condescended to teach the way; for this end He came from heaven. He hath written it down in a book. Give me that book! At any price, give me the Book of God!" John Wesley

Finally, I would like to say a word about the Bible. It is not a book, it is a library, a collection of 66 letters and books bound into one. These are the written testimonies of people who have had great supernatural experiences or visitations, and these are the written accounts or their first hand witness. Many archeological finds and historical writers validate much of scripture. Since the Bible speaks of a supreme authority, God, and His judgments and punishments for sin, many will try to discredit the existence of God and the validity of the Bible. Personally, with the supernatural experiences of my own life, I believe it completely. Let us begin.

CHAPTER 1
AUTHORITY OF SCRIPTURE

To begin any study on End Time events and sequence, a scholarly student of prophecy must begin with the ultimate authority on prophecy and that source of all sources – The Bible. As the foundational script of all that is to be given among men and believed, the validity and reliability of the Word of God should be our first focus.

First, I believe it is important to say that the Bible states truths that are provable, realistic, and true to life whether one believes in the God of the Bible or not. Absolute truth is true absolutely. History proves out and validates many of the prophecies that have already come to pass. Archeological artifacts support Biblical truth with empirical evidence. In this study, it is not our intent to prove the Bible, but to state what the Bible says about itself. This only works on the hungry. If one is not hungry to learn about and know God, then we would suggest one should sit back and watch history unfold. The Bible will prove itself in time.

John 12:48

He that rejecteth me, and receiveth not my words, that one that judgeth him: the word that I have spoken, the same shall judge him in the last day.

Probably at the top of the list called, "Important things to remember before leaving the earth" are the words Jesus speaks to us here. His words, whether we believe in Him or not, will judge us in the last day. Revelation gives us a snapshot of that day:

Revelation 20:12

And I saw the dead, small and great, stand before God; and the books were opened: and another book was opened, which is the book of life: and the dead were judged out of those things which were written in the books, according to their works.

God has a book written about each of our lives and He has His book that shows the way we must live for fullness of joy and happiness in Him. Any book that God will use to judge me should be the most important book in my life. For those of us who revere the word of God and follow His teachings, that day will be a great day of rejoicing. Christians believe what Peter states in 2 Peter 1:20, that prophecy came straight from God. A person of a legal mind would study the word intensely to know what he could hold God to, because if God has spoken it, He must perform it.

Yes, He did speak through men, through their personalities and life experiences. But they were moved by the Holy Spirit, that is the holy Spirit of God. For those who reject their one true Creator, the Bible does not mince words what the future holds for the ungrateful.

2 Thessalonians 2:10-13

And with all deceivableness of unrighteousness in them that perish; because they received not the love of the truth, that they might be saved. And for this cause God shall send them strong delusion, that they should believe a lie: that they all might be damned who believed not the truth, but had pleasure in unrighteousness. But we are bound to give thanks alway to God for you, brethren beloved of the Lord, because God hath from the beginning chosen you to salvation through sanctification of the Spirit and belief of the truth:

"The Truth" is spoken of as if there is only one truth, one way of salvation. Paul loved Timothy as his own son in the faith. He mentored and fathered Timothy in the ways of the Lord. Paul instructs Timothy:

2 Timothy 3:15-16

And that from a child thou hast known the holy scriptures, which are able to make thee wise unto salvation through faith which is in Christ Jesus. All scripture is given by inspiration of God, and is profitable for doctrine, for reproof, for correction, for instruction in righteousness;

Here it states emphatically that all scripture, yes, even though it was written down with the hand of man, is inspired by God Almighty and contains "the Truth" that will lead us into sound doctrine, good behavior and godly living. The word Bible comes from the Latin word biblios meaning the books or library. The Bible is 66 books compiled into one, a collection from the Spirit of God. The book of my life in heaven must be filled with those qualities of "the Truth" and sound doctrine if I am to make heaven my eternal home. I can rely on the word of God, the Bible, to lead me on a straight and narrow path to eternal life. Not only does the Bible testify of the Law and the Prophets, but all scripture points the way to the Messiah, the Saviour of the world, God in flesh - Jesus Christ.

John 5:39

Search the scriptures; for in them ye think ye have eternal life: and they are they which testify of me.

We see that again in Matthew as Jesus explains He did not come to make the Law null and void, but to live and teach it correctly. All was fulfilled in Jesus Christ, centuries of prophecies from men of God that did not know each other, that lived in different ages and cultures, yet spoke precisely about the day when the Messiah would come and what He would do.

Matthew 5:17-20

17 Think not that I am come to destroy the law, or the prophets: I am not come to destroy, but to fulfil.

18 For verily I say unto you, Till heaven and earth pass, one jot or one tittle shall in no wise pass from the law, till all be fulfilled.

19 Whosoever therefore shall break one of these least commandments, and shall teach men so, he shall be called the least in the kingdom of heaven: but whosoever shall do and teach them, the same shall be called great in the kingdom of heaven.

20 For I say unto you, That except your righteousness shall exceed the righteousness of the scribes and Pharisees, ye shall in no case enter into the kingdom of heaven.

So why should we study prophecy? First, prophecy lays a foundation for the certainty of what we believe. Focusing specifically on prophecy about Jesus Christ, no man could have set up all the fulfillments to scripture that Jesus fulfilled. Because of the consistency and accuracy of the prophecies over time and placement, as we have stated before, reliability of the Word of God is assured.

Prophecy establishes the certainty and absolute dependability of the Word. All things come to pass exactly as foretold – secular history bears this out. Some happened to the day of the foretelling, such as the Feasts of Israel which were also prophecies in their own right.

Prophecy tells us what to believe, the truth of the scripture, how to live this truth, where you are now in your personal walk with God in God's time clock, where you are going, and what manner of person God expects you to be. His counsel to stand firm with His grace and not be shaken is possible with the hope we see for God's people in prophecy. Lastly, but maybe the most important, prophecy gives us hope and assurance that God is in control and we can trust Him.

Who has believed our report? The Bible was written by several first hand eye witnesses. Pilate, in John 18:38, asked Jesus, "What is truth?" Being a Roman politician, we can understand his question.

Even Pilot's wife told him to have nothing to do with this righteous man.

Matthew 27:19

When he was set down on the judgment seat, his wife sent unto him, saying, Have thou nothing to do with that just man: for I have suffered many things this day in a dream because of him.

Pilot's wife was speaking truth to him, a first-hand witness of what God was telling her about this man named Jesus before Pilate judged Him. The Bible is the written testimonies of people's life experiences. Either we believe them, or we don't. Many authors over 3600 years of time have written the letters compiled into what is now our Bible. Can so many be wrong? 95% of the world's population believes in some form of supernatural deity. Are they all delusional? Paul's life was forever altered and he was willing to die for what he saw and heard. Men chosen to walk with Jesus saw Moses and Elijah speaking to him and they were also willing to die for what they saw and heard in just 3 ½ years. Paul, in his defense, said (1 Corinthians 15:6) in essence, "if you don't believe me, go ask the 500 that saw Him after His resurrection."

So now we would like to look at some famous people in the Bible that testified to the authenticity and authority of the Word of God. Throughout their lives, the witnesses staked their life, their family and their nation on the words out of the mouth of God. Each one's witness to those truths and God's faithfulness to His word which are recorded in the Bible.

The witness of David:

Psalm 91:4 "He shall cover thee with his feathers, and under his wings shalt thou trust: his truth shall be thy shield and buckler."

Psalm 119:11 "Thy word have I hid in mine heart, that I might not sin against thee."

Psalm 119:89 "Forever, O Lord, thy word is settled in heaven."

Psalm 119:105 "Thy word is a lamp unto my feet, and a light unto my path."

Psalm 119:160 "Thy word is true from the beginning: and every one of my righteous judgments endureth for ever."

Psalm 138:2 "I will worship toward thy holy temple, and praise thy name for thy lovingkindness and for thy truth: for thou hast magnified thy word above all thy name."

The witness of Solomon:

Proverbs 2:1-7 "My son, if thou wilt receive my words, and hide my commandments with thee; so that thou incline thine ear unto wisdom, and apply thine heart to understanding; Yea, if thou criest after knowledge, and liftest up they voice for understanding; If thou sleekest her as silver, and searchest for her as for hid treasures: then shalt thou understand the fear of the Lord, and find the knowledge of God."

Proverbs 4:5,7 "He taught me also and said unto me, Let thine heart retain my words: keep my commandments, and live. Wisdom is the principal thing; therefore get wisdom: and with all thy getting get understanding."

Proverbs 13:13 "Whoso despiseth the word shall be destroyed: but he that feareth the commandment shall be rewarded."

Proverbs 23:23 "Buy the truth, and sell it not; also wisdom, and instruction, and understanding."

The witness of Daniel:

Daniel 10:21 "But I will shew thee that which is noted in the scripture of truth: and there is none that holdeth with me in these things, but Michael your prince."

The witness of Matthew:

Matthew 5:18 "For verily I say unto you, till heaven and earth pass, one jot or one tittle shall in no wise pass from the Law, till all be fulfilled."

The witness of Mark:

Mark 7:13 "Making the word of God of none effect through your tradition, which ye have delivered: and many such like things do ye."

The witness of Luke:

Luke 4:4 "and Jesus answered him, saying, It is written, that man shall not live by bread alone, but by every word of God."

Luke 16:17 "And it is easier for heaven and earth to pass, than one tittle of the Law to fail."

Acts 17:11 "These were more noble than those in Thessalonica, in that they received the word with all readiness of mind, and searched the scriptures daily, whether those things were so."

The witness of John:

John 6:63 "It is the spirit that quickeneth; the flesh profiteth nothing:

the words that I speak unto you, they are spirit, and they are life."

John 17:17-19 "Sanctify them through thy truth: they word is truth. As thou hast sent me into the world, even so have I also sent them into the world. And for their sakes I sanctify myself, that they also might be sanctified through the truth. Neither pray I for these alone, but for them also which shall believe on me through their word."

1 John 2:14 "I have written unto you, fathers, because ye have known him that is from the beginning, I have written unto you, young men, because ye are strong, and the word of God abideth in you, and ye have overcome the wicked one."

The witness of Paul:

1 Corinthians 9:19-22 "For though I be free from all men, yet have I made myself servant unto all, that I might gain the more. And unto the Jews I became as a Jew, that I might gain the Jews; to them that are under the Law, as under the Law, that I might gain them that are under the Law; To them that are without Law, as without Law, (being not without Law to God, but under the Law to Christ,) that I might gain them that are without Law. To the weak became I as weak, that I might gain the weak: I am made all things to all men, that I might by all means save some.

Ephesians 4:11 "and he gave some, apostles; and some, prophets; and some, evangelists; and some, pastors and teachers;

Hebrews 4:12 "for the word of God is quick, and powerful, and sharper than any two-edged sword, piercing even to the dividing asunder of soul and spirit, and of the joints and marrow, and is a discerner of the thoughts and intents of the heart.

Ephesians 6:17 "And take the helmet of salvation, and the sword of the Spirit, which is the word of God

1 Thessalonians 1:5 "For our gospel came to you not in word only, but in power, in the Holy Ghost, in much assurance as you know what manner of men we were when we were among you for your sake."

2 Thessalonians 1:7-10 "And to you who are troubled rest with us, when the Lord Jesus shall be revealed from heaven with his mighty angels, in flaming fire taking vengeance on them that know not God, and that obey not the gospel of our Lord Jesus Christ: Who shall be punished with everlasting destruction from the presence of the Lord, and from the glory of his power; When he shall come to be glorified in his saints, and to be admired in all them that believe (because our testimony among you was believed) in that day.

2 Timothy 2:24-26 "And the servant of the Lord must not strive; but be gentle unto all men, apt to teach, patient, in meekness instructing those that oppose themselves; if God peradventure will give them repentance to the acknowledging of the truth; and that they may recover themselves out of the snare of the evil, who are taken captive by him at his will."

In the appendix, we have included a chart of the Old Testament and the New Testament divisions of the books. We hope the chart will help you to see how the Bible is divided into sections for a more meaningful study.

CHAPTER 2
SPRING FEASTS OF ISRAEL

In the Law of Moses, the first 5 books of the Bible, we learn about creation, about God's requirements for His creation, about God's dealings with man, about God's rules, and consequences. God spoke to Abraham in **Genesis 15:13-16:**

The Lord spoke to Abram, Know of a surety that thy seed shall be a stranger in a land that is not theirs and shall serve them. And they shall afflict them 400 years and also that nation, whom they shall serve, will I judge. And afterward they shall come out with great substance and thou shall go to thy fathers in peace and shalt be buried in a good old age. But in the fourth generation, they shall come hither again, for the iniquity of the Amorites is not yet full.

This is the prophecy that came to pass exactly as it was told to Abraham. According to the New Unger's Bible dictionary, under Amorites (page 54), Amorites is "a tribe descended from Canaan (Genesis 10:16) and one of the seven whose lands were given to

Israel...the Amorites were so prominent that their name seems sometimes to be used for Canaanites in general..." This statement of Genesis 15:16 sets a precedent that God will not bring judgment upon a people until their iniquity is "full." This means in the end time spoken of in Daniel 8:23, that states, "when the transgressors are come to the full..." meaning there is no further hope of repentance, so the Gentile Church will be removed. The Gentile nations can no longer repent, their hearts are fully set and their minds are made up to do evil and they cannot change, as it is when one is "set in their ways." God says that's enough and mercy stops.

When the children of Israel were brought out of Egypt, they came to Sinai where they were given the Law which contained in a hidden picture God's plan for the Jews and the rest of the world. God foretold the future of Abram's family, that in 400 years they would become a nation and come out with great substance. Then God would judge the nation that they served (Egypt) and Ammon (Canaan). This came to pass as it was told Abraham: 400 years after Joseph, they came out. This is an amazing example of God foretelling the future, and then bringing it to pass exactly as spoken.

There are two classes of people that prophecy concerns: the people God has attached Himself to, and the nations of the world that affect those people. Those are the only two kinds of people prophecy affects. We will see in Daniel the foretelling of specific future nations that would arise and their leaders. Were there other nations that were world powers also? Possibly in Africa, or other places? Sure. But these did not concern God's people, therefore they were not included in the holy Word from God.

When Israel was delivered from Egypt, there were some ritual Feasts that were set in order in the Law to commemorate great acts of deliverance that God had done for His people. The Feasts also, in a hidden form, foretell a future fulfillment. There are seven Feasts of significance mentioned in Leviticus 23.

Leviticus 23:5 – In the fourteenth day of the first month at even is the Lord's passover.

The first Feast in the Jewish celebration calendar with prophetic significance is the Feast of Passover. This Feast was inaugurated at the deliverance of Abraham's family from Egypt. We say they were not a nation yet, just a huge family group, possibly 2 million strong. They were not a nation because they did not have land. In order to be a nation, they would need land and a government, some sort of military defense and an economic understanding of the distribution of goods and services. Before Egypt, they were a hereditary nomadic shepherd clan. All of these other things they learned in Egypt. Moses was educated in the palace, so he learned politics, economy, military, and governance. He was the perfect leader. None of it was a mistake or happenstance. God's sovereignty is amazing.

The means of their deliverance from Egypt required a lamb without spot or blemish to be killed in the evening, to be eaten roast with fire and the blood of this lamb to be struck on the lintel and the door posts of each Israelite house. In order for the lamb and its blood to be efficacious, the Israelite had to remain in the house where the blood had been applied. The death angel would come and kill the first born male of man and beast where there was no blood on the dwelling. When the death angel came and saw the blood, he would pass over that house, and the inhabitants were spared. Merely killing the lamb and eating of it would not save them. Merely sprinkling the blood on the door posts still would not save unless they remained in the dwelling where they partook of the lamb with his blood on the door posts. For prophecy to work in our favor, we must fulfill all of its requirements. We must also understand that the events that are foretold in prophecy are valid and true because they are not left to circumstance or the hand of man. As sure as the death angel came, after nine plagues of witness, there were many that died in Egypt because they did not apply the blood of the lamb. Just believing the blood of the lamb was the substitutionary sacrifice was not enough. Just shedding the blood was not enough. One had to partake of the blood of the lamb, then take and apply it to their dwelling place and remain in the house.

Exodus 12:5-14, 22-33

5 Your lamb shall be without blemish, a male of the first year: ye shall take it out from the sheep, or from the goats:

6 And ye shall keep it up until the fourteenth day of the same month: and the whole assembly of the congregation of Israel shall kill it in the evening.

7 And they shall take of the blood, and strike it on the two side posts and on the upper door post of the houses, wherein they shall eat it.

8 And they shall eat the flesh in that night, roast with fire, and unleavened bread; and with bitter herbs they shall eat it.

9 Eat not of it raw, nor sodden at all with water, but roast with fire; his head with his legs, and with the purtenance thereof.

10 And ye shall let nothing of it remain until the morning; and that which remaineth of it until the morning ye shall burn with fire.

11 And thus shall ye eat it; with your loins girded, your shoes on your feet, and your staff in your hand; and ye shall eat it in haste: it is the Lord's passover.

12 For I will pass through the land of Egypt this night, and will smite all the firstborn in the land of Egypt, both man and beast; and against all the gods of Egypt I will execute judgment: I am the Lord.

13 And the blood shall be to you for a token upon the houses where ye are: and when I see the blood, I will pass over you, and the plague shall not be upon you to destroy you, when I smite the land of Egypt.

14 And this day shall be unto you for a memorial; and ye shall keep it a feast to the Lord throughout your generations; ye shall keep it a feast by an ordinance for ever.

22 And ye shall take a bunch of hyssop, and dip it in the blood that is in the bason, and strike the lintel and the two side posts with the blood that is in the bason; and none of you shall go out at the door of his house until the morning.

23 For the Lord will pass through to smite the Egyptians; and when he seeth the blood upon the lintel, and on the two side posts, the Lord will pass over the door, and will not suffer the destroyer to come in unto your houses to smite you.

24 And ye shall observe this thing for an ordinance to thee and to thy sons for ever.

25 And it shall come to pass, when ye be come to the land which the Lord will give you, according as he hath promised, that ye shall keep this service.

26 And it shall come to pass, when your children shall say unto you, What mean ye by this service?

27 That ye shall say, It is the sacrifice of the Lord's passover, who passed over the houses of the children of Israel in Egypt, when he smote the Egyptians, and delivered our houses. And the people bowed the head and worshipped.

28 And the children of Israel went away, and did as the Lord had commanded Moses and Aaron, so did they.

29 And it came to pass, that at midnight the Lord smote all the firstborn in the land of Egypt, from the firstborn of Pharaoh that sat on his throne unto the firstborn of the captive that was in the dungeon; and all the firstborn of cattle.

30 And Pharaoh rose up in the night, he, and all his servants, and all the Egyptians; and there was a great cry in Egypt; for there was not a house where there was not one dead.

31 And he called for Moses and Aaron by night, and said, Rise up, and get you forth from among my people, both ye and the children of Israel; and go, serve the Lord, as ye have said.

32 Also take your flocks and your herds, as ye have said, and be gone; and bless me also.

33 And the Egyptians were urgent upon the people, that they might send them out of the land in haste; for they said, We be all dead men.

The New Testament fulfillment tells us that Jesus Christ became our Passover lamb. He is the sinless substitute sacrifice. This is mentioned in Hebrews where the Word talks about Jesus Christ as our sin offering:

Hebrews 10:1-10

1 For the law having a shadow of good things to come, and not the very image of the things, can never with those sacrifices which they offered year by year continually make the comers thereunto perfect.

2 For then would they not have ceased to be offered? because that the worshippers once purged should have had no more conscience of sins.

3 But in those sacrifices there is a remembrance again made of sins every year.

4 For it is not possible that the blood of bulls and of goats should take away sins.

5 Wherefore when he cometh into the world, he saith, Sacrifice and offering thou wouldest not, but a body hast thou prepared me:

6 In burnt offerings and sacrifices for sin thou hast had no pleasure.

7 Then said I, Lo, I come (in the volume of the book it is written of me,) to do thy will, O God.

8 Above when he said, Sacrifice and offering and burnt offerings and offering for sin thou wouldest not, neither hadst pleasure therein; which are offered by the law;

9 Then said he, Lo, I come to do thy will, O God. He taketh away the first, that he may establish the second.

10 By the which will we are sanctified through the offering of the body of Jesus Christ once for all.

The Book of Hebrews also explains that a testament is only in force after one dies.

Hebrews 9:15-17

15 And for this cause he is the mediator of the new testament, that by means of death, for the redemption of the transgressions that were under the first testament, they which are called might receive the promise of eternal inheritance.

16 For where a testament is, there must also of necessity be the death of the testator.

17 For a testament is of force after men are dead: otherwise it is of no strength at all while the testator liveth.

18 Whereupon neither the first testament was dedicated without blood.

19 For when Moses had spoken every precept to all the people according to the law, he took the blood of calves and of goats, with water, and scarlet wool, and hyssop, and sprinkled both the book, and all the people,

Therefore, the New Testament came into force after the death and resurrection of Jesus Christ. In the Old Testament, to kill and partake of the lamb and application of the blood saved them from the death angel and also brought about the deliverance of God's people. This was a shadow picture of the New Testament. To partake of the death of Jesus Christ, we are buried in His name by water baptism.

Acts 2:38

Then Peter said unto them, Repent, and be baptized every one of you in the name of Jesus Christ for the remission of sins, and ye shall receive the gift of the Holy Ghost.

And we receive of His spirit in the likeness of His resurrection. The Old Testament prophecy said spirit birth would look like this:

Joel 2:28

28 And it shall come to pass afterward, that I will pour out my spirit upon all flesh; and your sons and your daughters shall prophesy, your old men shall dream dreams, your young men shall see visions:

Romans 6:3-4

3 Know ye not, that so many of us as were baptized into Jesus Christ were baptized into his death?

4 Therefore we are buried with him by baptism into death: that like as Christ was raised up from the dead by the glory of the Father, even so we also should walk in newness of life.

The blood of Jesus Christ is applied in water baptism in His name:

1 Peter 3:18-21

18 For Christ also hath once suffered for sins, the just for the unjust, that he might bring us to God, being put to death in the flesh, but quickened by the Spirit:

19 By which also he went and preached unto the spirits in prison;

20 Which sometime were disobedient, when once the longsuffering of God waited in the days of Noah, while the ark was a preparing, wherein few, that is, eight souls were saved by water.

21 The like figure whereunto even baptism doth also now save us (not the putting away of the filth of the flesh, but the answer of a good conscience toward God,) by the resurrection of Jesus Christ:

1 Corinthians 10:1-4

1 Moreover, brethren, I would not that ye should be ignorant, how that all our fathers were under the cloud, and all passed through the sea;

2 And were all baptized unto Moses in the cloud and in the sea;

3 And did all eat the same spiritual meat;

4 And did all drink the same spiritual drink: for they drank of that spiritual Rock that followed them: and that Rock was Christ

Colossians 2:11-15

11 In whom also ye are circumcised with the circumcision made without hands, in putting off the body of the sins of the flesh by the circumcision of Christ:

12 Buried with him in baptism, wherein also ye are risen with him through the faith of the operation of God, who hath raised him from the dead.

13 And you, being dead in your sins and the uncircumcision of your flesh, hath he quickened together with him, having forgiven you all trespasses;

14 Blotting out the handwriting of ordinances that was against us, which was contrary to us, and took it out of the way, nailing it to his cross;

15 And having spoiled principalities and powers, he made a shew of them openly, triumphing over them in it.

Colossians relates water baptism to circumcision, making circumcision an Old Testament prophetic picture of water baptism in the New Testament. One must remember when the Apostles preached New Testament salvation, they did it entirely from Old Testament scriptures. Consider the prophecies of Jesus Christ found in (KJV) Isaiah 53, Psalm 22, Zechariah 12 and 13. These speak in a hidden picture of the coming suffering Messiah. The first prophetic picture was given to Eve in the garden in Genesis 3:14-15. The serpent would bruise His heal, portraying the death of the Jesus Christ, heralding the coming of a suffering Messiah before a reigning Messiah. Eve was told that her "seed" would bruise the head of the serpent. A woman does not have seed, man has seed. So this was talking about a miracle birth, also spoken of in Isaiah 7:14, 9:6-7.

14 Therefore the Lord himself shall give you a sign; Behold, a virgin shall conceive, and bear a son, and shall call his name Immanuel.

Isaiah 9:6-7

6 For unto us a child is born, unto us a son is given: and the government shall be upon his shoulder: and his name shall be called Wonderful, Counsellor, The mighty God, The everlasting Father, The Prince of Peace.

7 Of the increase of his government and peace there shall be no end, upon the throne of David, and upon his kingdom, to order it, and to establish it with judgment and with justice from henceforth even for ever. The zeal of the Lord of hosts will perform this.

As in Egypt, merely "believing" that the lamb was a substitutionary sacrifice was not enough, in and of itself. Partaking of the lamb was not enough, but the lamb must be killed, roast with fire, eaten, and the blood applied to the three sides of the doorpost, and one must remain in the house until morning. In like manner, believing that Jesus is the substitutionary sacrifice alone is not enough. Merely praying a sinner's prayer of repentance is not complete in and of itself, but are part of the steps of salvation. In the New Testament, we believe Jesus is our atoning sacrifice. We pray a sinner's prayer of repentance and we apply the blood by water baptism in Jesus name, then receive His spirit with the scriptural evidence of speaking in other tongues as told in Acts 2:38.

Leviticus 23:6 – the Feast of Unleavened Bread was the second spring Feast. Exodus 12:15-20 mentions unleavened bread as a seven day observance, beginning on the second day after Passover and continuing for seven days. This cleansing of leaven out of their homes for seven days represents the life of a Believer who must be conscientious to cleanse themselves of sin from Passover, or partaking of the Lamb (repentance) to the completion of their life (number seven), lest they be cut off. So serious is the picture, that verse 19 concludes the matter, "...whosoever eateth that which is leavened, even that soul will be cut off from the congregation of Israel, whether he be a stranger or born in the land." Jesus Christ was crucified on Passover, was buried before the Sabbath and descended into hell to set captivity free. This is the "like figure" of water baptism which relates to the burial of the body of Jesus Christ, spoken of in 1 Peter 3:21. Passover represented His death, which was replicated in the Believer by repentance. A death to old lifestyle and self-governing. There are three applications of the blood in a New Testament believer's life, just as there were three applications to the door post in Egypt. The first application is death or repentance. To cleanse all the sin out of one's life is the second application of the blood. There were three on Passover: both sides of the door post and on the top. The picture in the New Testament is repentance, water baptism in Jesus name, the name of the Lamb, and the third, to receive His Spirit as stated in Acts 2:38. This process is the three applications of the blood of the Lamb.

1 John 5:8 says, "there are three that bear witness in the earth: the spirit, and the water and the blood. And these three agree in one." These are the three applications of the blood of the Lamb: the spirit is the infilling of the Holy Ghost, the water is water baptism, and the blood representing the death or repentance of the Believer.

Acts 2:38 is the first salvation message preached by anyone at the birth of the Church implementing the three applications of the blood. Repentance, water baptism in Jesus name, the name of the sacrificial Lamb, and the infilling of His spirit with the evidence of speaking in other tongues. For further study, look at (KJV) 1 Peter 3:21, Romans 6:3-4, Acts 8:12-17, Acts 10:44-48, Acts 19:1-6, 1 Corinthians 3:11, Acts 4:10-12, John 3:5-8, Mark 16:15-20, Luke 24:45-49.

We will pause here and mention a rule for symbols in Biblical interpretation, "the law of first mention." The first time a symbol is mentioned as portraying something, the scripture sets a precedent that carries throughout scripture. In this case, we are talking about leaven which is given a negative connotation at first mention, representing sin. Consider 1 Corinthians 5:4-13, where Paul mentions a "little leaven leavens the whole lump." Also, Matthew 16:12 where Jesus warns of the leaven of the Pharisees. So leaven is still negative even in the New Testament. For example, Matthew 13:33 states that "the Kingdom of Heaven is like leaven which a woman took and hid in three measures of meal until the whole was leavened." Generally speaking, anywhere in the Bible, a woman is a symbol either of Israel or the Church. Leaven, as we have stated previously, is a negative connotation representing sin, and it was hidden in three measures of meal. Leaven is used to raise bread dough and the Word of God is likened to bread or manna. Possibly this parable was not interpreted by Jesus because it referred to an event which would not happen until the Church was established. Leaven being negative, the three measures could represent how the woman manipulated the word of God. Because the Word speaks of God, one might conclude this parable is prophetic of the introduction of a three headed god-head which is never found in the Old Testament, and would be an adulteration of truth in the New Testament, especially since He stated continually in the Old Testament that He is one. Consider also, every Old Testament appearance of God was a singular being, sometimes accompanied by angels. Please refer to (KJV) Genesis 18:1-2, 22, 33, 19:1. This was God and two angels appearing to Abraham. Genesis 32:24-30 where God wrestles with Jacob. In Exodus 24:10-11, 33:9-11, God appeared to Moses and Israel as a singular being. Joshua 5:15, 6:2, here the Lord appears as the Captain of the Lord's host, speaking to Joshua (no angel ever told anyone to take off their shoes because the ground where they were standing was holy). Joshua 6:2 said "the Lord" said until Joshua... This tells us who was doing the talking. Isaiah 6:1-6, one

Lord on one throne with two six-winged Seraphim and Ezekiel 1:26-28, one man on one throne. These are all Old Testament appearances of God, a singular being. Thus, the parable of the woman and three measures was prophetic of the apostasy and idolatry which would happen.

Returning to our discussion of the Feast of Unleavened Bread, we are commanded by God to clean all of the sin out of our lives and our thoughts, beginning with the remission of all past sins in water baptism, and keeping ourselves free from the world through continual repentance and holy living. See (KJV) Romans 12:1-2, 2 Corinthians 7:1, and Hebrews 12:14. These are holy lifestyle scriptures.

Leviticus 23:10 – this was the third day after Passover, the Feast of Firstfruits. Exodus 23:10 tells us that they were to keep the Feast of the Firstfruits, the third Feast in a row to be kept when they entered the Promised Land. They were to bring the firstfruits of the land into the House of the Lord. This is a beginning harvest feast. The New Testament representation is that Jesus Christ rose from the dead and became the first to establish the new covenant which is the Church. Therefore, Jesus is the firstfruits of them that slept or were dead (1 Corinthians 15:20-23). Romans 8:23 states, "we which have received the Holy Ghost have the firstfruits of the Spirit." James 1:18 says we should be the firstfruits of His creatures. Romans 6:4 states we should rise (from water baptism, i.e. burial) to walk in newness of life (i.e.

resurrection). 1 Corinthians 15:20-23 states Christ rose from the dead and became the firstfruits of them that slept, or are asleep, because by man came death, by a man came also the resurrection of the dead. "For as in Adam all die, even so in Christ, shall all be made alive. But every man in his own order, Christ the first fruits, and afterward, they that are Christ's at His coming." Thus we see that without an understanding of the Old Testament feasts and their fulfillment, much of the feast terminology mentioned in the New Testament, which we have just shown, makes little sense. For further reading, see (KJV) Romans 6:5, Philippians 3:5, 2 Corinthians 4:6-14.

Romans 8:9-16 states that the Spirit of Christ in us, or the infilling of the Holy Ghost, is the power which will quicken our mortal bodies. In John 14:15-18, Jesus promises us the Holy Spirit, and tells us that He is the Holy Spirit, or Holy Ghost. When we receive the Holy Ghost, we receive the Spirit of Christ. John 20:22, Jesus commanded His disciples to receive the Holy Ghost. John 7:39 tells us the Spirit would not be given until after Jesus was glorified.

In summary of the first three Spring Feasts, each began on three consecutive days, representing the death, burial and resurrection of Jesus Christ, the Messiah. As we seek new birth, John 3:5, we must also experience the death (repentance), burial (water baptism in Jesus name) and resurrection (infilling of the Holy Ghost with evidence of speaking in tongues) to partake of the life of Christ. This is the "new birth".

Feast of Passover

Death of Jesus Christ   Our death through believing on the Lord Jesus Christ and repentance or turning away from a life of sin.

Feast of Unleavened Bread

Burial of Jesus Christ   Our burial through water baptism in the name of the Lord Jesus Christ.

Feast of Firstfruits

Resurrection of Jesus Christ   Our spiritual resurrection through the baptism of the Holy Ghost with the evidence of speaking in tongues.

Leviticus 23:15-22 – the last Spring Feast is the Feast of Pentecost, seven Sabbaths after the Feast of Firstfruits, or after 49 days. The next day, or the 50th day was the Feast of Pentecost. Leviticus 23:17 introduces an oddity. It commands us to bring two wave loaves of bread, baked with leaven! These are the only loaves ever baked and brought to the Tabernacle of the Law with leaven, which still represents sin. This is a type and shadow of the lives of Believers working in the harvest. We are the loaves with leaven. As long as we are in this world, in this sinful flesh, we are never saved by our own merit. Only by the blood of the Lamb are we saved, but we are set apart unto the work of the Lord throughout our lifetime. Some theologians have speculated that the two loaves could represent a rough time period of about two thousand years, meaning the age of the new covenant, or the Church age. Some think they represent the admittance of Jews and Gentiles into the new covenant. Since we have no clear scripture reference, we will make no definitive statement.

Pentecost began with a holy convocation and rest day. The New Testament fulfillment can be found in Acts 2:1, "When the day of Pentecost [meaning the Feast of] was fully come..." (brackets from author) This statement of scripture makes no sense without knowledge of the Old Testament prophetic feast. Fifty days after what? Why is it significant that the Day of Pentecost was fully come? The answer is that all four of the spring feasts were fulfilled on the month and day that it was prophesied, setting a precedent that we should expect the next three prophetic feasts (the fall feasts) to be fulfilled in like manner.

Jesus Christ rose from the dead and was seen of the leadership for 40 days.

Acts 10:38-42

38 How God anointed Jesus of Nazareth with the Holy Ghost and with power: who went about doing good, and healing all that were oppressed of the devil; for God was with him.

39 And we are witnesses of all things which he did both in the land of the Jews, and in Jerusalem; whom they slew and hanged on a tree:

40 Him God raised up the third day, and shewed him openly;

41 Not to all the people, but unto witnesses chosen before of God, even to us, who did eat and drink with him after he rose from the dead.

42 And he commanded us to preach unto the people, and to testify that it is he which was ordained of God to be the Judge of quick and dead.

1 Corinthians 15:6

6 After that, he was seen of above five hundred brethren at once; of whom the greater part remain unto this present, but some are fallen asleep.

At His ascension, He told the disciples to go to Jerusalem and they did that for 10 days, fasting and waiting for "the Promise", thus making 50 days ("pente" meaning 50). The first three Feasts were to show how to partake of the death, burial and resurrection of Jesus Christ. On the day of Pentecost, Peter and the others (120 souls in all) experienced new birth and Peter preached the death, burial and resurrection of the new Believer, commanding them to repent, be baptized in the name of Jesus Christ for the remission of sins and they would receive the gift of the Holy Ghost with the evidence of speaking in other tongues. Upwards of 3000 did so that same day, and the birth of the New Testament Church occurred. See Acts 2:38-40.

In the Old Testament, the Feast of Pentecost began with a holy convocation and a rest day. Isaiah 28:11-12 spoke of the outpouring of the Spirit with the result of speaking in other tongues as being the rest "wherewith the weary may rest, and the refreshing." In Acts 1:4-5, the resurrected Jesus commanded His leadership group to wait for the promise of the Father that they would be baptized with the Holy Ghost in a few days. The fulfillment came in Acts 2:1-4. Peter said, in Acts 2:16, "this is that which was spoken of by the prophet Joel. It shall come to pass in the last days, sayeth God, I will pour out of my spirit upon all flesh: and your sons and your daughters shall prophesy..." Therefore, we find Old Testament prophets foretelling of the New Testament outpouring of the Spirit and not even knowing it was linked to the Feast day, a day of celebration of harvest. In the original it was a celebration of a field harvest. In the New Testament, it is a celebration of a harvest of souls, God giving us back the spirit we lost in the Garden, making us complete in Him who is the Father incarnate:

Colossians 2:8-10

8 Beware lest any man spoil you through philosophy and vain deceit, after the tradition of men, after the rudiments of the world, and not after Christ.

9 For in him dwelleth all the fulness of the Godhead bodily.

10 And ye are complete in him, which is the head of all principality and power:

The number 50 is also tied to the year of Jubilee, every 50 years, when all debtors were released from their debts and whosoever had lost his inheritance due to debt, received it back in full. In like manner, all have lost their soul and are incapable of paying the debt to a holy

God. We have lost our inheritance, but thank God for Pentecost where a debtor can be released and go free, regaining his inheritance of eternal life.

Leviticus 25:10-13

10 And ye shall hallow the fiftieth year, and proclaim liberty throughout all the land unto all the inhabitants thereof: it shall be a jubilee unto you; and ye shall return every man unto his possession, and ye shall return every man unto his family.

11 A jubilee shall that fiftieth year be unto you: ye shall not sow, neither reap that which groweth of itself in it, nor gather the grapes in it of thy vine undressed.

12 For it is the jubilee; it shall be holy unto you: ye shall eat the increase thereof out of the field.

13 In the year of this jubilee ye shall return every man unto his possession.

We, as debtors to sin, have our sins remitted in baptism and receive our inheritance, lost in the Garden, given back to us in an abundant life here and eternal life to come. Hebrews 10:1 tells us the Law had a shadow of good things to come, and not just the image of those things. The sacrifices of the Old Testament could not save us, but pointed us to the ultimate sacrifice of the sinless Christ to the saving of our souls. Leviticus 23:22 speaks of provision for the non-Jew. In the story of Ruth, God had already provided in His Law a way for the poor and the "stranger", or non-Jew, to partake in the harvest given to Israel.

Ruth was a foreigner, a Moabite, an enemy to the Jews, but she desired to join herself to the God of the Israelites. She married a kinsmen to Naomi, her mother-in-law and became a part of the lineage of Jesus Christ through Boaz, great grandfather to King David. Boaz himself was son to Rahab the harlot, another non-Jew who saved the two spies in Jericho, who was spared when she was given a scarlet thread to hang in her window by the two spies. The promise was given to her that when they brought death to Jericho, all who were in her house, with the scarlet thread, would be spared. But if any went out, their blood was on their own head. This was a symbol again of the blood of the Lamb on the door post that spared from the death angel in Egypt. Rahab did this and was accepted into the tribe of Judah through marriage. Leviticus 23:22 gives the Gentile hope that we can be part of the harvest of souls to the New Jerusalem.

Leviticus 23:22

22 And when ye reap the harvest of your land, thou shalt not make clean riddance of the corners of thy field when thou reapest, neither shalt thou gather any gleaning of thy harvest: thou shalt leave them unto the poor, and to the stranger: I am the Lord your God.

Also, in the New Testament, Paul states that he was ordained an apostle to the Gentiles following the call of the Lord telling us that provision was made for the Gentiles to also be included in God's harvest of souls in the New Testament. Indeed, the scripture states, when Mary and Joseph took Jesus on the eighth day to be circumcised according to the Law of Moses, they were met by a man named Simeon at the temple. The Bible tells us of this man, that the Lord had promised him he would not die until he had seen the Lord's Christ. The story continues, when Simeon saw Jesus in His mother's arms, took Him in his own arms and declared, "A light to lighten the Gentiles and the glory of thy people Israel." Some references that have shown Gentiles would be included are:

Isaiah 9:1c-2

1c ...and afterward did more grievously afflict her by the way of the sea, beyond Jordan, in Galilee of the nations.

2 The people that walked in darkness have seen a great light: they that dwell in the land of the shadow of death, upon them hath the light shined.

Isaiah 49:6

6 And he said, It is a light thing that thou shouldest be my servant to raise up the tribes of Jacob, and to restore the preserved of Israel: I will also give thee for a light to the Gentiles, that thou mayest be my salvation unto the end of the earth.

Matthew 4:14-15

14 That it might be fulfilled which was spoken by Esaias the prophet, saying,

15 The land of Zabulon, and the land of Nephthalim, by the way of the sea, beyond Jordan, Galilee of the Gentiles;

CHAPTER 3
FALL FEASTS OF ISRAEL:
THE BEGINNING OF END TIME PROPHECY

The Feast of Pentecost closed Israel's springtime festivals. Following Pentecost, there would be four long summer months during which the next harvest would be allowed to ripen and then reaped before the next holy day which is the Feast of Trumpets. Prophetically, the summer months after the spring are for growth for the next harvest of souls in the Church. We are now in that period where God is growing His Church and bringing all things to pass for the end time unfolding drama.

Leviticus 23:23-25 – This is the Feast of Trumpets, or Rosh Hashanah. It is the first fall feast. It is a day of rest, a sacred assembly, celebrated with trumpet blasts. The command was, "you shall do no regular work, but present an offering made by fire unto the Lord."

This day also is celebrated as the Jewish New Year. Israel had several calendars, some Rabbis have mentioned four. For our purposes, there are two: the civil calendar which began in the month of Nisan, and the religious calendar which began in the month of Tishri. One of the best known Jewish customs for New Years day is the greeting, "May you be inscribed for a New Year!" This is based on the belief that God judges the world each year on Rosh Hashanah.

The Mishna, which is the written code of the oral law, speaks of this as a day of judgment when all men pass before the Creator and are examined as a shepherd examines his sheep. Many Rabbis also believe that the first of Tishri is the date of creation. Some important points: the harvest was reaped before the Feast of trumpets blew. The trumpets were blown at the first sign of the appearing of the new moon, therefore this feast occurs at night, and there was an offering made by fire unto the Lord. The New Testament fulfillment is the rapture, or catching away of spirit filled saints to meet the Lord in the air. It would be the beginning of the new year for the Jewish people because the next feasts would begin the remainder of their new life.

1 Thessalonians 4:13-18

13 But I would not have you to be ignorant, brethren, concerning them which are asleep, that ye sorrow not, even as others which have no hope.

14 For if we believe that Jesus died and rose again, even so them also which sleep in Jesus will God bring with him.

15 For this we say unto you by the word of the Lord, that we which are alive and remain unto the coming of the Lord shall not prevent them which are asleep.

16 For the Lord himself shall descend from heaven with a shout, with the voice of the archangel, and with the trump of God: and the dead in Christ shall rise first:

17 Then we which are alive and remain shall be caught up together with them in the clouds, to meet the Lord in the air: and so shall we ever be with the Lord.

18 Wherefore comfort one another with these words.

A student of the Bible will conclude this feast anticipates a pre-tribulation rapture of saints, before God pours out His judgment on the earth. Consider the two Old Testament examples of rapture: Enoch (Genesis 5:24, Hebrews 11:5), and Elijah (2 Kings 2:11).

Matthew, in his gospel 3:11, says, "I indeed baptize you with water unto repentance. But He that cometh after me is mightier than I, whose shoes I am not worthy to bear. He shall baptize you with the Holy Ghost and with fire, whose fan is in His hand, and He will thoroughly purge His floor and gather His wheat into the garner. But He will burn up the chaff with unquenchable fire." This scripture speaks of harvest and an offering made by fire, which relates to Pentecost and the Feast of Trumpets. Also, in Acts 2:3-4, cloven tongues of fire sat on each of them, signifying that it is an offering made by fire unto the Lord, the Jews being able to identify the Pentecost tongues of fire with the burning bush and the fire on the top of Mt. Sinai when God spoke.

The Feast of Trumpets happens on the "new moon" which is 29.5 days after the last new moon, meaning it might occur on the 29th or 30th day, occurring sometime between September and October. The Jewish calendar, a lunisolar calendar, does not follow the Gregorian calendar, the calendar most of us use, that follows a set number of days, so no one knows for sure. (www.biblprophesy.org/introtumpets.htm, retrieved June 28, 2014)

Matthew 24:36 – 42

36 But of that day and hour knoweth no man, no, not the angels of heaven, but my Father only.

37 But as the days of Noe were, so shall also the coming of the Son of man be.

38 For as in the days that were before the flood they were eating and drinking, marrying and giving in marriage, until the day that Noe entered into the ark,

39 And knew not until the flood came, and took them all away; so shall also the coming of the Son of man be.

40 Then shall two be in the field; the one shall be taken, and the other left.

41 Two women shall be grinding at the mill; the one shall be taken, and the other left.

42 Watch therefore: for ye know not what hour your Lord doth come.

Of all the Feasts, this is the only one that is set by the appearance of the new moon.

Luke 21:34 - 36

34 And take heed to yourselves, lest at any time your hearts be overcharged with surfeiting, and drunkenness, and cares of this life, and so that day come upon you unawares.

35 For as a snare shall it come on all them that dwell on the face of the whole earth.

36 Watch ye therefore, and pray always, that ye may be accounted worthy to escape all these things that shall come to pass, and to stand before the Son of man.

The fullness of Gentiles mentioned in Romans 11 is talking about the Church: "until the fullness of the Gentiles be come in." The times of the Gentiles in Luke 21:24 is talking about the end of Gentile kingdoms or the beast that Daniel and John in Revelation both saw, the one world governmental system and its ruler. There is a difference between the Rapture, or catching away of the Church, and the second coming of the Lord.

At this point we need to explain about trumpets and their significance in Prophecy. Numbers 10:1-10 the Lord commanded to make two trumpets of silver: one for the calling of the assembly, and one for the journeying of the camp. Additionally, they were used to blow an alarm of war (v.9) and blow over their burnt offerings (v.10). These trumpets are not the ram's horn, Shofar, neither are they judgment trumpets. This is where many teachers of end time prophecy are confused, because, when we get into Revelation, there are seven judgment trumpets. The Bible says we shall be raised from the dead at the last trumpet:

1 Thessalonians 4:16

16 For the Lord himself shall descend from heaven with a shout, with the voice of the archangel, and with the trump of God: and the dead in Christ shall rise first:

1 Corinthians 15:52

52 In a moment, in the twinkling of an eye, at the last trump: for the trumpet shall sound, and the dead shall be raised incorruptible, and we shall be changed.

These are not the Revelation trumpets. The first trumpet sounds for the gathering of the camp – May 14,, 1948, Israel became a nation. The second trumpet is for the journeying of the camp. Israel will not be ready to journey then, so this trumpet is for the journeying of the Church, which is a natural branch of Judaism as Jesus is the Jewish Messiah and the Bible was written by Jewish writers. The Church is made up of spiritual Jews.

Romans 2:28-29

28 For he is not a Jew, which is one outwardly; neither is that circumcision, which is outward in the flesh:

29 But he is a Jew, which is one inwardly; and circumcision is that of the heart, in the spirit, and not in the letter; whose praise is not of men, but of God.

Now, let us refer to **Mark 13:28-33.**

28 Now learn a parable of the fig tree; When her branch is yet tender, and putteth forth leaves, ye know that summer is near:

29 So ye in like manner, when ye shall see these things come to pass, know that it is nigh, even at the doors.

30 Verily I say unto you, that this generation shall not pass, till all these things be done.

31 Heaven and earth shall pass away: but my words shall not pass away.

32 But of that day and that hour knoweth no man, no, not the angels which are in heaven, neither the Son, but the Father.

33 Take ye heed, watch and pray: for ye know not when the time is.

Jesus is speaking of the nation of Israel in the parable of the fig tree. He states that this generation shall not pass until all things be fulfilled. We know that in B.C. 582, Nebuchadnezzar raised Solomon's Temple and took away everything except the four sacred pieces of the inner chamber made by Moses for the Holy Place and the Holy of Holies. The four sacred pieces have never been recovered. In A.D. 70, the Emperor Titus raised the second Temple in Jerusalem (Zerubabbel's Temple built during the end of the Old Testament and remodeled by Herod) and scattered the Jews abroad throughout all the earth. The new, young fig tree of Israel did not put forth its leaf again until May

14, 1948 when Israel again became an independent nation. Not since the Babylonian captivity has Israel been independent (582 B.C.). Jesus mentions of the day and the hour, knows no man.

Matthew 24:36

36 But of that day and hour knoweth no man, no, not the angels of heaven, but my Father only.

This relates to the Feast of Trumpets which falls on a different day and hour every year, although it is always in the fall and usually between the end of September and the first of October. 1 Thessalonians 5:1-10 is a huge end time dissertation by Paul, the apostle with the PhD. In chapter 4:13-17, Paul mentions the resurrection/rapture. In verse 16, he says,

16 For the Lord himself shall descend from heaven with a shout, with the voice of the archangel, and with the trump of God: and the dead in Christ shall rise first:

This trumpet is blown in heaven at the Feast of Trumpets. On May 14, 1948, prophetically, the first trumpet blew for the calling of the assembly establishing the camp, gathering the Jews from all corners of the world for the first time since Christ, back into their own land, reestablishing them as a nation.

Jeremiah 29:14-15

14 And I will be found of you, saith the Lord: and I will turn away your captivity, and I will gather you from all the nations, and from all the places whither I have driven you, saith the Lord; and I will bring you

again into the place whence I caused you to be carried away captive.

Jeremiah 31:10

10 Hear the word of the Lord, O ye nations, and declare it in the isles afar off, and say, He that scattered Israel will gather him, and keep him, as a shepherd doth his flock.

Ezekiel 11:17-20

17 Therefore say, Thus saith the Lord God; I will even gather you from the people, and assemble you out of the countries where ye have been scattered, and I will give you the land of Israel.

18 And they shall come thither, and they shall take away all the detestable things thereof and all the abominations thereof from thence.

19 And I will give them one heart, and I will put a new spirit within you; and I will take the stony heart out of their flesh, and will give them an heart of flesh:

20 That they may walk in my statutes, and keep mine ordinances, and do them: and they shall be my people, and I will be their God.

Zechariah 7:13-14

13 Therefore it is come to pass, that as he cried, and they would not hear; so they cried, and I would not hear, saith the Lord of hosts:

14 But I scattered them with a whirlwind among all the nations whom they knew not. Thus the land was desolate after them, that no man passed through nor returned: for they laid the pleasant land desolate.

Zechariah 8:20-23

20 Thus saith the Lord of hosts; It shall yet come to pass, that there shall come people, and the inhabitants of many cities:

21 And the inhabitants of one city shall go to another, saying, Let us go speedily to pray before the Lord, and to seek the Lord of hosts: I will go also.

22 Yea, many people and strong nations shall come to seek the Lord of hosts in Jerusalem, and to pray before the Lord.

23 Thus saith the Lord of hosts; In those days it shall come to pass, that ten men shall take hold out of all languages of the nations, even shall take hold of the skirt of him that is a Jew, saying, We will go with you: for we have heard that God is with you.

Covenant promises throughout the major and minor prophets declare that in the last days, people shall come up to the House of the Lord in Jerusalem. Some Old Testament scriptures tell us this is following the battle of Armageddon. (See KJV Joel 3:9-21). So God's intension has been to return the Jews to their land all along. There will be much war until the end, but in the end, the true Jew wins. Not those that are only hereditary, but those who are practicing, Word keeping, Jehovah worshipping, Messiah anticipating Jews. Israel, we pray for you.

However, since the Hebrew Jew has not accepted Jesus Christ as that Messiah yet, then he who has converted already to Judaism through the means of the Church is the one that is ready.

The next trumpet that will blow will be the journeying of the camp, or the rapture. So let us ask a question: who is the Church? Are they a separate religion from Israel? Or are they a bridge from the old covenant to the new? The answer is also found in **Hebrew 12:22-29** where Paul says,

22 But ye are come unto mount Sion, and unto the city of the living God, the heavenly Jerusalem, and to an innumerable company of angels,

23 To the general assembly and Church of the firstborn, which are written in heaven, and to God the Judge of all, and to the spirits of just men made perfect,

24 And to Jesus the mediator of the new covenant, and to the blood of sprinkling, that speaketh better things than that of Abel. [italics added]

Jesus is the mediator of the new covenant, i.e. the Church. Our God is a Jewish Messiah.

25 See that ye refuse not him that speaketh. For if they escaped not who refused him that spake on earth, much more shall not we escape, if we turn away from him that speaketh from heaven:

26 Whose voice then shook the earth: but now he hath promised, saying, Yet once more I shake not the earth only, but also heaven.

27 And this word, Yet once more, signifieth the removing of those things that are shaken, as of things that are made, that those things which cannot be shaken may remain.

28 Wherefore we receiving a kingdom which cannot be moved, let us have grace, whereby we may serve God acceptably with reverence and godly fear:

29 For our God is a consuming fire.

John 1:10-13

10 He was in the world, and the world was made by him, and the world knew him not. (God in Christ).

11 He came unto his own, and his own received him not. (Hebrew people)

12 But as many as received him, to them gave he power to become the sons of God, even to them that believe on his name: (the Church)

13 Which were born, not of blood, nor of the will of the flesh, nor of the will of man, but of God.

We see by these New Testament references that the Church is the spiritual adopted children into the promises of God which were originally given to the Hebrew children. This, then, makes us heirs of the prophecies and eternity.

Romans 2:28-29

28 For he is not a Jew, which is one outwardly; neither is that circumcision, which is outward in the flesh:

29 But he is a Jew, which is one inwardly; and circumcision is that of the heart, in the spirit, and not in the letter; whose praise is not of men, but of God.

Therefore, the promises of the Law fall to both camps because the Church is the natural branch of Judaism, provided it professes allegiance to the singular one God of the Old Testament and not a plurality of Greek mythology which crept into Christian doctrine around 325 A.D.

Interpreters of prophecy sometimes become confused on the interpretation of words such as "works", "saints" as well as "trumpets." Romans speaks of works of the Law while James speaks of works of faith. Sometimes in the gospels Jesus is speaking to the Jewish nation. At other times He is speaking to the disciples as the heads of the new Church. Sometimes the word "saints" is referring to Old Testament peoples and sometimes it is referring to New Testament spirit filled people and in Revelation, there are Tribulation saints that come out of the Jewish nation and are put under the altar to await a time period. These are separate groups of people. Salvation for the Gentiles will be closed at the culmination of the Feast of Trumpets. **Romans 11:25** says,

"I would not, brethren, that you should be ignorant of this mystery lest you should be wise in your own conceits, that blindness in part has happened to Israel until the fullness of the Gentiles be come in." (Conceits are thoughts.)

The word "fullness" is number 4138 in Thayer's Greek/English Lexicon of the New Testament, meaning "full number." It is safe to presume that no Gentile can be saved after the full number has already been saved or raptured. Therefore, there is no "Left Behind" series!

Micah 5:3

3 Therefore will he give them up, until the time that she which travaileth hath brought forth: then the remnant of his brethren shall

return unto the children of Israel.

This Old Testament prophecy in Micah confirms Paul's words of Romans 11. It was God's intention from the beginning to take out a Church and then return to natural Israel afterwards.

The remaining Feasts of prophecy are left to Israel to bring them to revelation, repentance and acceptance of Jesus Christ as their Messiah. Zechariah 12:10 says, "...they shall look upon me whom they have pierced and they shall mourn for Him as one mourneth for his only son..." Please notice the "me" is a "him." In other words, the Old Testament God took on the form of man. Note also Zechariah 13:6 which says, "One shall say unto him, what are these wounds in thine hands? And he shall answer, those which I was wounded in the house of my friends." Also, Matthew 23:38-39 where Jesus says, "Your house is left unto you desolate, for I say unto you, you shall not see me henceforth until you shall say, blessed is He that cometh in the name of the Lord."

Colossians 2:8-10

8 Beware lest any man spoil you through philosophy and vain deceit, after the tradition of men, after the rudiments of the world, and not after Christ.

9 For in him dwelleth all the fulness of the Godhead bodily.

10 And ye are complete in him, which is the head of all principality and power:

The Old Testament God dwelt in the human form of Jesus Christ. See also KJV John 14:8-10. Of that day we do not know times or days, but we do know seasons. John 9:4 says we must work while it is day and Jesus said, "I must work the works of Him who sent me while it is still day because the night comes when no man can work." Jesus was back handedly referring to the Feast of Trumpets, which is the only night occurring Feast in which no work can be done because the harvest is complete and it is now dark. Several scriptures state that we are not ignorant of the times and seasons. Jesus spoke of this, Paul spoke of it and Peter spoke of it. It is obvious to know when the end of harvest is. It is obvious to know when you are leaving summer and coming into fall. It is obvious when the harvest is over, because there is no more grain to get. Then it is time to put the harvest into the bin and prepare for the next season. Many of Israel's Feasts commemorate just such occasions. These natural celebrations, such as growth season and harvest, also represent spiritual celebrations. There will be a time when the Gentile harvest is complete. This will be culminated with the harvest of the Gentile Church, then God will humble the Gentile nations, thus bringing Israel to repentance and ushering in the Millennium.

Jesus said not one jot or tittle shall pass from the Law until all be fulfilled (a jot or tittle are embellishments upon the letters of the written Hebrew language. They are very, very small). Since the Feast of Trumpets is the next prophetic Feast to occur, one would have to conclude that at least part of the Law is still intact. The ceremonial and sacrificial parts of the Law were fulfilled in Jesus Christ. But the moral law is still in effect. It is still wrong to commit adultery. It is still wrong to steal. Prophecies made in the Law are still, some of them, yet to come to pass. Three fourths of the New Testament are direct quotes of the Old Testament. Without the foundation and knowledge of the Old Testament we really have no groundwork for understanding the New Testament. These Feasts are alluded to over and over in the New Testament. For example, Jesus is the firstfruits of them that slept.

1 Corinthians 15:20-23

22 For as in Adam all die, even so in Christ shall all be made alive.

23 But every man in his own order: Christ the firstfruits; afterward they that are Christ's at his coming.

Without the Feast of Firstfruits in the Old Testament, we would not understand the significance of what is meant by "firstfruits". Consider that the New Testament salvation was preached using Old Testament scriptures, as much of the New Testament was not written until later. Consider the analogy in **1 Corinthians 10:1-4**.

1 Moreover, brethren, I would not that ye should be ignorant, how that all our fathers were under the cloud, and all passed through the sea;

2 And were all baptized unto Moses in the cloud and in the sea;

3 And did all eat the same spiritual meat;

4 And did all drink the same spiritual drink: for they drank of that spiritual Rock that followed them: and that Rock was Christ.

The deliverance from Egypt is a type of New Testament salvation. Paul said, "They were all baptized unto Moses in the cloud and in the sea." Thus portraying that we are all baptized unto Jesus in the water and in the spirit.

2 Peter 3:8-14

8 But, beloved, be not ignorant of this one thing, that one day is with the Lord as a thousand years, and a thousand years as one day.

9 The Lord is not slack concerning his promise, as some men count slackness; but is longsuffering to us-ward, not willing that any should perish, but that all should come to repentance.

10 But the day of the Lord will come as a thief in the night; in which the heavens shall pass away with a great noise, and the elements shall melt with fervent heat, the earth also and the works that are therein shall be burned up.

11 Seeing then that all these things shall be dissolved, what manner of persons ought ye to be in all holy conversation and godliness,

12 Looking for and hasting unto the coming of the day of God, wherein the heavens being on fire shall be dissolved, and the elements shall melt with fervent heat?

13 Nevertheless we, according to his promise, look for new heavens and a new earth, wherein dwelleth righteousness.

14 Wherefore, beloved, seeing that ye look for such things, be diligent that ye may be found of him in peace, without spot, and blameless.

All that God has pronounced will occur. No thing or no one can stop Him: not the devil, not humanity, not any in creation. Whether prophecy about the world or prophecy in our personal lives, God will perform it. We can't stop it.

CHAPTER 4
REMAINING FALL FEASTS OF ISRAEL

Leviticus 23:27-32 Feast of Reconciliation - Day of Atonement or Yom Kippur. A brief quote of explanation from a reliable source will begin our study through this feast:

"The Day of Atonement was [observed] in Jerusalem. This was the one day of the year that the High Priest entered into the Holy of Holies to bring the yearly blood sacrifices for the covering of Israel's sins. This was a day of reconciliation, as Israel humbly came before Jehovah God, confessing their transgressions. Since the Day of Atonement was the great day of cleansing from sin, it was not meant to be a joyous celebration, but a sober place where death lurked, and new life began. The High Priest, carefully following the exact words of instruction from the word of God, prepared himself to walk before a holy God. Israel came fasting and afflicting their souls, actually moaning and repenting over their sinful ways." (Dugas, P.D. (1983) The Feasts of Jehovah in Prophecy. Portland, OR: Apostolic Book Publishers).

(Also see Edersheim, A. The Temple: its ministry and services, p. 268-269).

Pastor Dugas has explained the essence of that Feast and what transpired on that holy day once per year. The blood of the sacrificial perfect lamb was sprinkled on the Tabernacle furniture (Golden Candlestick, the Table of Shewbread, and the Altar of Incense), then the High Priest entered into the Holiest of Holies and sprinkled the blood on the Mercy Seat and Ark of the Covenant. Once this was done, the Shekinah glory of God would descend upon the camp as God accepted this sacrifice and covered the sins of Israel one more year as found in Leviticus 16:1-34.

Leviticus 16:16-19 (KJV)

16 And he shall make an atonement for the holy place, because of the uncleanness of the children of Israel, and because of their transgressions in all their sins: and so shall he do for the tabernacle of the congregation, that remaineth among them in the midst of their uncleanness.

17 And there shall be no man in the tabernacle of the congregation when he goeth in to make an atonement in the holy place, until he come out, and have made an atonement for himself, and for his household, and for all the congregation of Israel.

18 And he shall go out unto the altar that is before the Lord, and make an atonement for it; and shall take of the blood of the bullock, and of the blood of the goat, and put it upon the horns of the altar round about.

19 And he shall sprinkle of the blood upon it with his finger seven times, and cleanse it, and hallow it from the uncleanness of the children of Israel.

In the New Testament, Jesus Christ is our sacrificial Lamb without spot and blemish. He is also the High Priest of our profession (Hebrews 3:1), meaning our religion, our lifestyle, our daily walk with God, a profession of our faith. In the Old Testament it required a High Priest to perform the sacrifices and cleansing of the Temple, the Altar and the people. The High Priest was before the face of all the people when they repented. In order for Israel to fulfill this prophetic day in the end time, their High Priest must be visible and present to cleanse the Temple, the Altar and the people. It is important to note that Israel has been unable to keep this Day of Atonement as it requires a High Priest, a Temple, and the acceptable sacrifices which have not existed for 2000 years. See also, Daniel 9:24-27 which speaks of "seventy sevens which are determined upon the holy city and the people of Israel to finish the transgression, to make an end of sins, to make reconciliation for iniquity and to bring in everlasting righteousness..." This tells us the Day of Atonement cannot occur until the end of the seven year Great Tribulation because that is the remaining "week" of seven years prophesied in Daniel. We will explain this when we cover Daniel. Suffice it to say now, that the next prophetic feast following Trumpets/Rapture does not occur until the end of the Tribulation period which is also known as Jacob's trouble:

Jeremiah 30:7

7 Alas! for that day is great, so that none is like it: it is even the time of Jacob's trouble; but he shall be saved out of it.

Even though the Jews may think Jacob's Trouble was World War II and the Holocaust, woe upon woe is yet to come. So we should pray for the peace of Jerusalem.

Psalm 122:6

6 Pray for the peace of Jerusalem: they shall prosper that love thee.

Matthew 24:29-31 gives us a picture of the events immediately following the battle of Armageddon and the return of Jesus Christ when Jesus appears and physically sets His foot on the Mt. of Olives with ten thousands of His saints. We will discuss this in depth when we present end time in the Book of Revelation. See also Zechariah chapters 12 - 14, Joel 2:29-32 and Ezekiel 37. Israel will see their Messiah and repent. The Mt. of Olives will cleave in two, waters will issue forth, and the Dead Sea will be healed. Jude 14-15 tells us, "And Enoch also, the seventh from Adam, prophesied of these, saying, Behold, the Lord cometh with ten thousands of His saints, to execute judgment upon all, and to convince all that are ungodly among them of all their ungodly deeds which they have ungodly committed, and all their hard speeches which ungodly sinners have spoken against Him." If Jesus is going to return with ten thousands of His saints, those saints would first have been taken to meet Him, thus implying a pre-tribulation rapture.

Once the Day of Atonement has been prophetically fulfilled, the Gentile armies that came against Israel will have been destroyed. Then the way is prepared for the fulfillment of the next feast which is the Feast of Tabernacles or Booths.

Leviticus 23:34-44 Feast of Tabernacles or Booths. The Feast of Tabernacles was instituted by the Lord to be celebrated when they came into the land of Israel and had rest from their enemies. This is a feast of rejoicing. It was kept seven days. This was to commemorate when they were brought out of Egypt and they were made to dwell in booths, or tents throughout the wandering in the wilderness under Moses. God brought them into their own land and gave them rest from their enemies, and delivered them from their bondage. Its prophetic fulfillment will occur at the end of the Great Tribulation period. After the Lord Jesus Christ has been revealed as the conquering and reigning Messiah, that He will dwell in the midst of them one thousand years.

All seven of these feasts were instituted for two purposes: first, to remind Israel of the deliverances that God had wrought, and also the blessings that God had given. God wanted Israel to understand and remember and teach their children how much God had loved them, He chose them and set them apart specifically as a special people unto Himself, full of blessings, power, miracles, and wonder. And to show

His love for mankind, the feasts speak of what is yet to come, what God will do, the love He will show, the deliverance He will work and the miracles that are yet to be seen. The feasts demonstrate God's faithfulness in that even though the Jewish nation has rejected their Messiah, He is still determined to fulfill His promises that they shall yet say, "Blessed is He who comes in the name of the Lord." So we need to pray for our Jewish friends, for much pain and woe is coming their direction.

Matthew 24:29- 31

39 And knew not until the flood came, and took them all away; so shall also the coming of the Son of man be.

40 Then shall two be in the field; the one shall be taken, and the other left.

41 Two women shall be grinding at the mill; the one shall be taken, and the other left.

This is further prophesied in Zechariah 2:10-13, 3:10 and also Ezekiel 47 and Isaiah 66:10-24. This is a time of rejoicing and ingathering of God's people. Gentile nations will have been judged and Gentile rule in this world will have ended. God will establish a new world capital out of Jerusalem. After many emperors of Gentile nations which afflicted their will upon the world, the world will now see a righteous Emperor and will know such peace as it has not known since the Garden of Eden. In Revelation we will be discussing the frightening devastation that is wreaked upon the earth, so the population of the world will be greatly decimated. But the Law will come out of Mt. Zion during the Millennium and all will be healed and live in peace for a thousand years. Therefore the Feast of Tabernacles relates to the deliverance of Israel from the bondage of the Gentile nations that ruled over them and were brought into their own land and given rest, which will happen again in greater glory during the Millennium reign of Jesus Christ.

This concludes our study of the seven prophetic Feasts of Israel. Of great significance is the times and seasons when these Feasts occurred on the Jewish calendar. The Spring Feasts have been fulfilled and the Fall Feasts are yet to be. The Church of Jesus Christ awaits its own Rosh Hashanah or rapture, as it is commonly called, to take us out of this world. God will then turn His attention back to Israel to perfect her and cleanse her of all iniquity, thus completing the cycle of redemption.

Leviticus gave us an outline of prophetic events. How that plays out for the Jewish people will be further revealed in Daniel and Revelation. How that plays out for God's people and the Church will be told in the early part of Revelation with references to the Gospels and the Epistles. In our study of Revelation, we will complete the timeline of events, and bring everything to an end as God makes a people for His name to live forever in eternity. We will now turn our attention to the Book of Daniel.

DENNIS & LINDA KROG

CHAPTER 5
THE BOOK OF DANIEL

The reason prophecy works is because God declares to His prophets what will come to pass. See reference in **Isaiah 46:9-10**:

9 Remember the former things of old: for I am God, and there is none else; I am God, and there is none like me,

10 Declaring the end from the beginning, and from ancient times the things that are not yet done, saying, My counsel shall stand, and I will do all my pleasure

He declares the end from the beginning. So the end is already made known to us, it is not a mystery. Before the event comes to pass, He tells it in **Isaiah 48**:

3 I have declared the former things from the beginning; and they went forth out of my mouth, and I shewed them; I did them suddenly, and they came to pass.

4 Because I knew that thou art obstinate, and thy neck is an iron sinew, and thy brow brass;

5 I have even from the beginning declared it to thee; before it came to pass I shewed it thee: lest thou shouldest say, Mine idol hath done them, and my graven image, and my molten image, hath commanded them.

See also Amos 4:13 – He declares unto man what is His thought. He states He will tell us before it comes to pass. Thus we read of amazing prophecies in the Book of Daniel, God wanting Israel and the world to know spectacular events long before they happen, so we will put our trust in God, not man.

Due to the sins of Judah, the southern kingdom, they were taken captive by the king of Babylon in 582 B.C. In the second year of the king of Babylon, whose name is Nebuchadnezzar, God gave this king a dream. The interpretation is found in **Daniel 2:31-45**.

31 Thou, O king, sawest, and behold a great image. This great image, whose brightness was excellent, stood before thee; and the form thereof was terrible.

32 This image's head was of fine gold, his breast and his arms of silver, his belly and his thighs of brass,

33 His legs of iron, his feet part of iron and part of clay.

34 Thou sawest till that a stone was cut out without hands, which smote the image upon his feet that were of iron and clay, and brake them to pieces.

35 Then was the iron, the clay, the brass, the silver, and the gold, broken to pieces together, and became like the chaff of the summer threshing floors; and the wind carried them away, that no place was found for them: and the stone that smote the image became a great mountain, and filled the whole earth.

36 This is the dream; and we will tell the interpretation thereof before the king.

37 Thou, O king, art a king of kings: for the God of heaven hath given thee a kingdom, power, and strength, and glory.

38 And wheresoever the children of men dwell, the beasts of the field and the fowls of the heaven hath he given into thine hand, and hath made thee ruler over them all. Thou art this head of gold.

39 And after thee shall arise another kingdom inferior to thee, and another third kingdom of brass, which shall bear rule over all the earth.

40 And the fourth kingdom shall be strong as iron: forasmuch as iron breaketh in pieces and subdueth all things: and as iron that breaketh all these, shall it break in pieces and bruise.

41 And whereas thou sawest the feet and toes, part of potters' clay, and part of iron, the kingdom shall be divided; but there shall be in it of the strength of the iron, forasmuch as thou sawest the iron mixed with miry clay.

42 And as the toes of the feet were part of iron, and part of clay, so the kingdom shall be partly strong, and partly broken.

43 And whereas thou sawest iron mixed with miry clay, they shall mingle themselves with the seed of men: but they shall not cleave one to another, even as iron is not mixed with clay.

44 And in the days of these kings shall the God of heaven set up a kingdom, which shall never be destroyed: and the kingdom shall not be left to other people, but it shall break in pieces and consume all these kingdoms, and it shall stand for ever.

45 Forasmuch as thou sawest that the stone was cut out of the mountain without hands, and that it brake in pieces the iron, the brass, the clay, the silver, and the gold; the great God hath made known to the king what shall come to pass hereafter: and the dream is certain, and the interpretation thereof sure.

The king saw a huge statue of a man. The head was of pure gold, the arms and chest were of silver, the thighs were of brass, the two legs were of iron, and the feet were of iron and clay mixed. God gave the interpretation of the king's dream to the great prophet Daniel. This was concerning one world dictator rulership focusing on the Hebrew people. Two countries were not mentioned to the king because they existed before him. For reference of world powers, see the Reese Chronological Bible, which lists Egypt as the first world power from 1600 – 1200 B.C. and Assyria the second world power from 750 – 612 B.C. Our image from the dream begins with Babylon which would be the third world power from 612 – 539 B.C. The fourth kingdom would be the empire of the Medes and Persians (two arms equals two kingdoms) from 539 – 333 B.C. The fifth world power was Greece from 333 – 63 B.C. The sixth world power was Rome from 63 B.C. to 476 A. D. The seventh and final kingdom will be the ten kingdom alliance (ten toes) of the antichrist.

Daniel 9:26 mentions a prince that will come and shall destroy the city and the sanctuary in Jerusalem.

26 And after threescore and two weeks shall Messiah be cut off, but not for himself: and the people of the prince that shall come shall destroy the city and the sanctuary; and the end thereof shall be with a flood, and unto the end of the war desolations are determined.

The first fulfillment of Daniel's prophecy was Titus in A.D. 70. The second will be the antichrist. These kingdoms mentioned in the dream grow weaker from head to foot, as represented by inferior metals. In the last days, the image is smote on the feet by a stone cut out of the mountain. The mountain is Zion, the stone is Jesus Christ which will bring an end to Gentile world rule.

Matthew 21:44

44 And whosoever shall fall on this stone shall be broken: but on whomsoever it shall fall, it will grind him to powder.

The kingdom that will follow will be the Millennium reign or the kingdom of Jesus Christ. What is interesting is that at the time of this written prophecy, Babylon was the ruling empire. All of the other kingdoms have since come to pass, in succession, as they were presented in the king's dream.

In Daniel 7, Daniel has a dream where he sees a beast rise up out of the sea. The following images correspond with Nebuchadnezzar's image. Daniel 7:4, the first beast was like a lion and had eagle's wings, which, was the symbol of Babylon. Daniel said, "I beheld till the wings were plucked. It was lifted up from the earth and was made to stand upon the feet as a man and a man's heart was given to it." This is "the man" that Nebuchadnezzar saw in his dream. The second beast was like a bear (7:5). It raised up on one side, meaning, the Persians were stronger than the Medes. It had three ribs in its mouth and said, "Arise and devour much flesh." This tells of the fierceness and the cruelty of these nations. The third kingdom was like a leopard which had on the back of it four wings of a fowl and also four heads and dominion was given to it. This represents Alexander the Great who conquered the then known world, but at his early death, his kingdom was divided among his four generals, which are as follows:

A. Egypt, Libya, and Palestine controlled by Ptolemy

B. Asia was controlled by Seleucus (Antiochus IV Epiphanes from 175 – 163 B.C. was a Syrian king and a type of the antichrist.

C. Greece/Macedonia was controlled by Cassander

D. Asia Minor and Thrace was controlled by Lysimachus.

The four wings and the four heads are the same. The fourth beast is described as being dreadful and terrible, strong exceedingly having great iron teeth. It had ten horns and among those horns came up a little horn that plucked up three of the first ten, and it had a mouth speaking great things. This corresponds to the kingdom of the antichrist which will have ten kingdoms and its rulers, three will plucked up by the roots (7:8). Antiochus Epiphanes was a foreshadowing of the type of person and deeds that the antichrist will do.

The two legs of iron represent the Eastern and Western hemispheres of the Roman Empire. Daniel 7:9 says, in the culmination, the thrones will be cast down and the "Ancient of Days" will sit, whose description matches that of Jesus Christ in the Book of Revelation. The Bible interprets itself, if you read enough as we see in Daniel 7:16, it was made known unto him the interpretation of these things. These great beasts are four great kings, which shall rise out of the earth. Many waters, or the sea, usually means many peoples or nations. Verse 18 tells the outcome which says, "The saints of the most High shall take the kingdom and possess the kingdom forever." Verses 19 – 28 talks of the Roman Empire and the antichrist. We will address the end time Roman Empire, or the ten toes mixed with iron and clay, when we study the Book of Revelation.

In Daniel 8, we are told a second vision was given to Daniel which follows Nebuchadnezzar's image. In verse 3, he sees a ram with two horns and one horn was higher than the other which came up last. Verse 4 tells us that it was mighty and none could stand before him. This is the kingdom of the Medes and Persians. In verse 5, as Daniel was considering the last vision, a he-goat came from the west and did not touch the ground, and had a notable horn between his eyes. Verses 5 – 8 tells us the goat became very great, and moved with such speed that he didn't even touch the ground, because he conquered the world so fast. This is Alexander the Great and Greece. Verse 8 tells us that when he was strong, he became broken and in his place arose up four others, again this is speaking of his four generals as we have said before. Verses 9-12 speak of a horn that comes up among the first four which magnifies himself against the daily sacrifice and casts it to the ground. This was Antiochus Epiphanes. What is very interesting to note, at the time of Daniel's writing, none of these people even existed. Alexander the Great conquered the known world and died suddenly at a very young age of swamp fever. Greece was then divided among his four generals. So precise was Daniel's vision foretelling the nations and the leaders, written before it ever came to pass, that if we are not astounded, it is because we choose not to look, as these events were nothing less than miraculous as they occurred. So we see that history is not left to happenstance, but all things will come to pass as God has revealed.

Amos 3:7

7 Surely the Lord God will do nothing, but he revealeth his secret unto his servants the prophets.

This should give comfort to the people of God, and to the wise, it should give instruction for preparation. What manner of lives ought we to live?

Again, in verse 20, we are told the two horns are Media and Persia. God left nothing to guess. In verse 21, we are told the rough goat is the king of Grecia, and the great horn between his eyes is the first king (Alexander). Verse 22 says the first horn was broken, and four horns stood up in its place being the four generals or kingdoms that come from that nation. Verse 23 says in the latter time of their kingdom, when the transgressors are come to the full, a king of fierce countenance and understanding dark sentences shall stand up. This is the antichrist. After Daniel received an understanding of the vision, the Bible says he fell very sick for many days. Such dark foreboding would sicken anyone!

In Daniel 9:2, Daniel understood when he read **Jeremiah 25:11-16**:

11 And this whole land shall be a desolation, and an astonishment; and these nations shall serve the king of Babylon seventy years.

12 And it shall come to pass, when seventy years are accomplished, that I will punish the king of Babylon, and that nation, saith the Lord, for their iniquity, and the land of the Chaldeans, and will make it perpetual desolations.

13 And I will bring upon that land all my words which I have pronounced against it, even all that is written in this book, which Jeremiah hath prophesied against all the nations.

14 For many nations and great kings shall serve themselves of them also: and I will recompense them according to their deeds, and according to the works of their own hands.

15 For thus saith the Lord God of Israel unto me; Take the wine cup of this fury at my hand, and cause all the nations, to whom I send thee, to drink it.

16 And they shall drink, and be moved, and be mad, because of the sword that I will send among them.

Verse 12 says the number of the years of captivity would be 70, in compliance with the Law of Leviticus 26:32-35.

32 And I will bring the land into desolation: and your enemies which dwell therein shall be astonished at it.

33 And I will scatter you among the heathen, and will draw out a sword after you: and your land shall be desolate, and your cities waste.

34 Then shall the land enjoy her sabbaths, as long as it lieth desolate, and ye be in your enemies' land; even then shall the land rest, and enjoy her sabbaths.

35 As long as it lieth desolate it shall rest; because it did not rest in your sabbaths, when ye dwelt upon it.

The number 70 was the number of Sabbath years that Israel refused to keep the commandment in the Law. They were so greedy, that they refused to allow the land to rest every seventh year, thereby destroying the typology that the Sabbath was meant to portray. God removed them and gave the land rest to restore the Sabbath. This typology shows that following the seven year Tribulation, will come Israel's Sabbath, representing the thousand years of peace. Moses couldn't enter into the Promised Land because he messed up the typology of Christ when he smote the rock for water a second time when he was instructed of God to speak to the rock. The first time was typology of Christ smitten on Calvary and poured forth the water of the Spirit on the day of Pentecost. Since then, we are to speak to the rock as Christ will never again be smitten but we are to ask, seek and knock as in Luke 11, and we will receive the Spirit. God's typology is precious and cannot be messed with.

So Daniel saw there were 70 years determined on Israel's captivity from Jeremiah's prophecy. In Daniel 9:21, the angel Gabriel came to Daniel to give him further understanding and revelation. In verse 24, we are told 70 "weeks" are determined on thy people and the holy city. The word "weeks" is translated from the Hebrew word Heptad, which simply means seven. So it should read more correctly, seventy sevens are determined, which add up to 490 years. Verse 25 says, "Know and understand that from the going forth of the commandment to restore and rebuild Jerusalem, unto Messiah the Prince shall be seven weeks and three score and two weeks" which equals 69 weeks which is 483 years until Messiah. So Daniel knew exactly when Jesus Christ was to appear, and so did anyone who read Daniel. Some Rabbis have said that he also knew from the creation days that it would be 4000 years from creation as the greater light appeared on the fourth day and the Bible says one day is as a thousand and a thousand as one day to the Lord. Some have even speculated that Daniel, being a very rich man but having no children, saved his massive wealth, spanning several kings of Babylon and Persia, and left instructions to the wise men, of which he was chief, as to what year the Messiah would come and to watch during that time for a sign of His birth. Thus, the wise men of Jesus' time traveled for approximately 18 months to find the Christ child living in a house with his mother and Joseph, to give Him gifts that were probably suggested and set aside by Daniel for his Messiah that he knew would come and when. How else would pagan wise men know to bring gold, for His kingship, frankincense to honor His priesthood, and myrrh to honor His sacrifice? An ancient prophet in the area of Babylon left a prophecy also, recorded in Numbers 24:15-19 that a star shall arise out of Jacob and a scepter shall arise out of Israel, therefore leaving the wise men a clue to watch the heavens for a sign and a place as the stars were put there as signs of the glory of God.

Genesis 1:14

14 And God said, Let there be lights in the firmament of the heaven to divide the day from the night; and let them be for signs, and for seasons, and for days, and years:

Not only was the year prophesied, but also the place in Micah 5:1-6 which was going to be in Bethlehem, foretelling the birth of King David as well as Jesus Christ. How could they possibly miss it? The reason is they were offended, because there are scriptures that promise a ruling and reigning Messiah, i.e. the One of the Millennium, but He first came as a suffering Messiah which is also portrayed in scripture to the befuddlement of many rabbis. Some believe there would be two

Messiahs because of difference in the prophecies: one of a lowly birth, ending in death, and the other in the conquering Messiah and great victory and glory. We also can miss the truth of prophecy, unless we are willing to be honest and read it for what it says, not what we want it to say.

Micah 5:1-6

1 Now gather thyself in troops, O daughter of troops: he hath laid siege against us: they shall smite the judge of Israel with a rod upon the cheek.

2 But thou, Bethlehem Ephratah, though thou be little among the thousands of Judah, yet out of thee shall he come forth unto me that is to be ruler in Israel; whose goings forth have been from of old, from everlasting.

3 Therefore will he give them up, until the time that she which travaileth hath brought forth: then the remnant of his brethren shall return unto the children of Israel.

4 And he shall stand and feed in the strength of the Lord, in the majesty of the name of the Lord his God; and they shall abide: for now shall he be great unto the ends of the earth.

5 And this man shall be the peace, when the Assyrian shall come into our land: and when he shall tread in our palaces, then shall we raise against him seven shepherds, and eight principal men.

6 And they shall waste the land of Assyria with the sword, and the land of Nimrod in the entrances thereof: thus shall he deliver us from the Assyrian, when he cometh into our land, and when he treadeth within our borders.

They couldn't miss it. How did Israel not know? Jesus told the Pharisees, "You know who I am!" (John 7:28-29). The date of this commandment is found in Nehemiah 2:1, the month of Nissan, in the twentieth year of Artaxerxes the King, which was the 14th day of March, 445 B.C. The day when Jesus rode into Jerusalem, as Messiah the Prince, was Palm Sunday, April 2nd, 30 A. D., as told in Luke 19:37-40, fulfilling that prophecy almost to the day. With proof like this, how did they miss the Messiah? Israel, we shall weep for thee. But Israel shall accept Jesus Christ as their Messiah and that day is described in

Micah 4:1-7

1 But in the last days it shall come to pass, that the mountain of the house of the Lord shall be established in the top of the mountains, and it shall be exalted above the hills; and people shall flow unto it.

2 And many nations shall come, and say, Come, and let us go up to the mountain of the Lord, and to the house of the God of Jacob; and he will teach us of his ways, and we will walk in his paths: for the law shall go forth of Zion, and the word of the Lord from Jerusalem.

3 And he shall judge among many people, and rebuke strong nations afar off; and they shall beat their swords into plowshares, and their spears into pruninghooks: nation shall not lift up a sword against nation, neither shall they learn war any more.

4 But they shall sit every man under his vine and under his fig tree; and none shall make them afraid: for the mouth of the Lord of hosts hath spoken it.

5 For all people will walk every one in the name of his god, and we will

walk in the name of the Lord our God for ever and ever.

6 In that day, saith the Lord, will I assemble her that halteth, and I will gather her that is driven out, and her that I have afflicted;

7 And I will make her that halted a remnant, and her that was cast far off a strong nation: and the Lord shall reign over them in mount Zion from henceforth, even for ever.

A glorious day for our God and Savior, Jesus Christ. If you ever wondered if God cares about your family and their salvation, look at the efforts He has gone through and will cause to happen to save His own family. Will He do less for you? And may we put this question to you? Are the Jews the only family of God? Are not the descendants of Ishmael, Ammon and Moab also kin? Ishmael was the son of Abraham, Moab and Ammon the sons of Lot. Will He not reveal Himself to them also?

In verse 26 of Daniel 9, it says after three score and two weeks, which equals 69, shall Messiah be cut off but not for Himself, meaning Messiah will be crucified for our sins. This leaves one seven year period of judgment remaining upon the Hebrew people and Jerusalem. The prophet did not know about the 2000 year gap for the Gentile Church age, because his vision was only concerning the Jewish people. Verse 26 tells us further that the people of the Prince that shall come, i.e. Roman people, Emperor Titus, shall destroy the city and the sanctuary which occurred in A.D. 70. Verse 27 tells us of a Prince (antichrist) that shall come and shall confirm the covenant (of a peace plan) with many for one week or the remaining seven year period. This verse further tells us in the midst of the week, or 3 ½ years, he shall cause the sacrifice in the third temple to cease, telling us that out of the Tribulation period, the final 3 ½ years will be terrible. Returning to Daniel 8:25, it says he shall destroy many by peace. The covenant is one of peace but a deceitful peace, also spoken in Revelation 6:2, which we will discuss later in the Revelation chapter.

Daniel 11 is of importance because we can look back at that prophecy and find it in history. God is in control of world events. Herein is a summary of the scripture and its fulfillment through the eyes of history:

11:3-4 These verses speak of Alexander the Great. The scripture says, "When he shall stand up..." gives a hint that his reign might be brief because it says his kingdom shall be broken. Through history we know that Alexander fought the Persians at Granicus in 334 A.D. and the final Persian overthrow took place in 331 at Gaugamela. (See Youtube for a documentary about these battles and Alexander). Alexander then moved eastward toward Afghanistan and India through his conquest. Worn and tired, they all returned to Babylon in 327, so, in roughly eight years, he conquered the then known world but died in Babylon in 323 of swamp fever.

11:5-6 The verse mentions the "King of the South" or Egypt, whom we know to be Ptolemy I, or Soter, one of Alexander's generals. There were about 280 years between Ptolemy I and Cleopatra who died around 30 B.C. Ptolemy I died in 285 B.C., his son Ptolemy II, also known as Philadelphus, arranged a peace treaty with Antiochus II, also known as Theos. The two struck a bargain in which Antiochus, king of the north (in the dynasty of another general of Alexander in Syria), was to marry Berenice, the daughter of Ptolemy II. This is foretold in verse 6, "the king's daughter of the South shall come to the king of the North to make an agreement. But she shall not retain the power of the arm." The Bible predicts that she will not retain power, or her husband. In fact, Antiochus II already had a wife that he divorced. Being a powerful woman, she overthrew both of them, killing Berenice and her son, and later poisoning Antiochus. After which, she took the throne. So the prophecy was fulfilled, telling of the exact persons.

11:7-12 The branch of her roots (Berenice's brother, Ptolemy III) came against the king of the north (Assyria) to avenge his sister's murder. Ptolemy won and decimated the capitol of Assyria and then returned to Egypt victorious.

The rest of chapter 11 is fascinating from a historical point of view as it is a dissertation concerning what would come to pass among the four heads of the leopard after Alexander's death. This is the process of what would occur among Alexander's four generals of which his great kingdom was divided, kind of like the rest of the story. We will not discuss further detail of Chapter 11, to save space in this book. However, if you would like to study more, consult Youtube documentaries, Google, Daniel 11 timelines, also consult encyclopedias, and the Expositor's Bible Commentary. The overall important point we wish to make is that all of this world history was foretold to Daniel long before it came to pass, involving many rulers and many countries with marriages, and overthrows and military campaigns. All came to pass exactly as foretold. This can be a little scary or extremely comforting, depending how we view it.

It is our opinion, Daniel's greatest revelation was the time frame of the coming of the Messiah. No wonder he fell sick for many days and was in astonishment at what had been shown him. His 21 days of fasting reaped a harvest never to be imagined, yet one of sorrow. "Unto them was given the oracles of God" (Romans 3:1-2).

CHAPTER 6
THE RAPTURE TICKET TO RIDE

We are going to begin by saying this is the Book of the Revelation of Jesus Christ. Many call this "Revelations" but that is not true. It is a singular revelation to show His servants what must come to pass. What will be revealed in this book is Jesus Christ. First, to the Church, second to the Gentile nations, and third, to the remnant of Israel. There is a blessing just for reading this book found in Chapter 1, verse 3: "Blessed is he that readeth". A direct quote of Zechariah 12:10 is given in **Revelation 1:7**:

7 Behold, he cometh with clouds; and every eye shall see him, and they also which pierced him: and all kindreds of the earth shall wail because of him. Even so, Amen.

In this is a synopsis of the three stages of the revelation to mankind: first He comes with clouds – this is revelation to the Church which shall be caught up to meet Him in the air. Next is to the Jews, which turned Him over to be pierced and thirdly, the Gentile nations which are all the "kindreds of the earth." **Revelation 1:8**, Jesus speaking:

8 I am Alpha and Omega, the beginning and the ending, saith the Lord, which is, and which was, and which is to come, the Almighty.

He makes this statement again in chapter 4:8, 21:6, and 22:13. He is called the Lord Almighty, which was, which is and is to come. Chapters 2 and 3 are written to the seven Churches of Asia Minor which covered the broad base of the existing Church at that time. Interesting to note, He gave them praise for what they had correct, but they were told to repent of what was incorrect, and threatened with judgment if they did not. John, who was the prophet receiving this revelation, is afterward called up into heaven in the beginning of chapter 4 to "come and see." The word "Church" is not used again in the rest of the book after chapter 3. John sees one throne in heaven and one sitting on the throne. Jesus is proclaimed to be the Lord God Almighty, which was, which is, and is to come. There are beasts and 24 elders round about the throne. Verse 10 of chapter 5 says:

10 And hast made us unto our God kings and priests: and we shall reign on the earth.

5 Ye also, as lively stones, are built up a spiritual house, an holy priesthood, to offer up spiritual sacrifices, acceptable to God by Jesus Christ.

This coupled with a huge multitude mentioned in chapter 5:11, represents the Church which was called out of this world into heaven, thus ending the Church age. The remainder of this book is about the remaining 7 years or 70th week of Daniel, bringing an end to Gentile kingdoms and to bring Israel to repentance, to accept their Messiah, and to usher in the 1000 years of peace. From chapter 6 on, Revelation is not written in chronological order. To this most the Bible scholars agree.

Chapter 6:17 mentions the great day of His wrath. The seven seals that the Lamb breaks contain the wrath of God that He is going to pour out on this earth because they will not repent. Chapter 15:1, 7 tell me the seven vials are full of the wrath of God. Also chapter 16:1 says the same thing about the seven vials. All throughout the Bible, God's people have been spared from His wrath when judgment came and the end of one covenant was completed and a new covenant was brought forth. Consider Enoch who was raptured in Genesis 5:24, because he please God, so God scooped him up to heaven, and Noah who was spared from the wrath to come in Genesis 1:16. When God poured out His judgment upon the earth, He delivered the righteous first. In the case of Sodom and Gomorrah, Genesis 19:22-24, 29 tells us that God would not pour out the wrath on those two sinful cities until the righteous were delivered from it. Man has had to endure the wrath of man throughout all of time. The Church has had to endure the wrath of man and evil governments, but not the wrath of God. Paul said,

1 Thessalonians 1:10 - And to wait for his Son from heaven, whom he raised from the dead, even Jesus, which delivered us from the wrath to come.

1 Thessalonians 5:9 - For God hath not appointed us to wrath, but to obtain salvation by our Lord Jesus Christ,

Romans 2:5-10 - But after thy hardness and impenitent heart treasurest up unto thyself wrath against the day of wrath and revelation of the righteous judgment of God;

6 Who will render to every man according to his deeds:

7 To them who by patient continuance in well doing seek for glory and honour and immortality, eternal life:

8 But unto them that are contentious, and do not obey the truth, but obey unrighteousness, indignation and wrath,

9 Tribulation and anguish, upon every soul of man that doeth evil, of the Jew first, and also of the Gentile;

10 But glory, honour, and peace, to every man that worketh good, to the Jew first, and also to the Gentile:

Romans 5:9 - Much more then, being now justified by his blood, we shall be saved from wrath through him.

These scriptures speak of wrath upon those that are non-repentant, but glory, honor and peace to those that obey the truth. Romans 2:8 also mentions those that do not obey "the truth."

2 Thessalonians 1:7-8

7 And to you who are troubled rest with us, when the Lord Jesus shall be revealed from heaven with his mighty angels,

8 In flaming fire taking vengeance on them that know not God, and that obey not the gospel of our Lord Jesus Christ:

The remainder of the Book of Revelation from chapter 6 to the end is about the wrath of God upon those that did not obey the truth and did not obey the gospel.

There are many Christian denominations, each saying a different thing about salvation, how to be saved. Paul was emphatic about the word "doctrine" and the phrase, "the Truth." Jesus Himself, in John 4:22-24 tells us that we need to know what we worship. Jesus here validates to the woman at the well that Jews religion is where salvation came from. Furthermore, He said, "we know what we worship," stating the Jewish concept of God was correct. In verse 23, Jesus says, "true worshippers must worship the Father in spirit and in truth." So we need to ask ourselves a few questions: what was the Old Testament Jewish concept of the godhead, because Jesus said it was correct! What does it mean to worship in spirit and in truth? What are the Bible definitions of those terms?

Matthew 7:21-29 tells us that not everyone that calls Jesus "Lord" will enter into heaven. In verse 22, a group of religious people are described who claim to have prophesied in His name, cast out devils in His name and done wonderful works in His name, to whom He says in verse 23, "I never knew you. Depart from Me ye who work iniquity." He proceeds to tell us in verse 24, a righteous person is one that hears His words and does them. Sounds pretty strict. Is eternity something we should base on what we believe? Should we lightly think that God is required to accept whatever we give Him? Or should we, out of fear and respect for the Lord, search His book out to see what the requirements are? Is my concept of "believing" what the Bible defines as believing? Is believing that Jesus Christ existed enough? Is praying the "sinner's prayer" enough?

John, in his gospel, chapter 3:5-8 says:

5 Jesus answered, Verily, verily, I say unto thee, Except a man be born of water and of the Spirit, he cannot enter into the kingdom of God.

6 That which is born of the flesh is flesh; and that which is born of the Spirit is spirit.

7 Marvel not that I said unto thee, Ye must be born again.

8 The wind bloweth where it listeth, and thou hearest the sound thereof, but canst not tell whence it cometh, and whither it goeth: so is every one that is born of the Spirit.

Please note in verse 5, Jesus plainly states, unless you are born of the water and born of the spirit, you CANNOT enter the kingdom of God. Verse 8 tells me, for everyone that is born of the spirit, there is a sound.

Mark 16:15-18

15 And he said unto them, Go ye into all the world, and preach the gospel to every creature.

16 He that believeth and is baptized shall be saved; but he that believeth not shall be damned.

17 And these signs shall follow them that believe; In my name shall they cast out devils; they shall speak with new tongues;

18 They shall take up serpents; and if they drink any deadly thing, it shall not hurt them; they shall lay hands on the sick, and they shall recover.

Verses 15 and 16 tells us that the gospel includes a believer's baptism. So how is it that some denominations preach that water baptism is not necessary? Why lie? Verse 17 tells us that gospel also includes power over devils, speaking in tongues, and laying hands on the sick with results. These signs shall follow Believers that obey the gospel. He said, "these signs shall follow them that believe IN MY NAME." If these signs are not common in your church, maybe they are not preaching "the Truth" of "the gospel."

Luke 24:46-49

46 And said unto them, Thus it is written, and thus it behoved Christ to suffer, and to rise from the dead the third day:

47 And that repentance and remission of sins should be preached in his name among all nations, beginning at Jerusalem.

48 And ye are witnesses of these things.

49 And, behold, I send the promise of my Father upon you: but tarry ye in the city of Jerusalem, until ye be endued with power from on high.

Read Acts 2:1-4 to see how it happened. What does "endued with power" look and sound like?

These scriptures tell us that repentance and remission of sins are preached in His name. Peter in Acts 2:38 says that water baptism is in the name of the Lord Jesus Christ for, or unto, the remission of sins. In Luke 24:29, Jesus commanded them to wait in Jerusalem for the promise of the spirit. This would be the fulfilling of the birth of water and spirit He spoke of in John 3. Acts 1:4-5 says that Jesus spoke of the promise of the baptism of the Holy Ghost ten days from then. Here comes the birth of the spirit – what did it look like? What did it sound like? Jesus said in John 3:8, everyone born of the spirit would make a sound. Jesus said in Mark 16, believers would speak with new tongues. Joel 2:28 and Isaiah 28:1 and 12 both prophesy of it. **Acts 2:1-4** tells what the birth of the spirit looked like on the day of Pentecost.

1 And when the day of Pentecost was fully come, they were all with one accord in one place.

2 And suddenly there came a sound from heaven as of a rushing mighty wind, and it filled all the house where they were sitting.

3 And there appeared unto them cloven tongues like as of fire, and it sat upon each of them.

4 And they were all filled with the Holy Ghost, and began to speak with

THE FINAL STORY

other tongues, as the Spirit gave them utterance.

In Acts 2:16, the apostle Peter said that this was the fulfillment of **Joel 2:28.**

28 And it shall come to pass afterward, that I will pour out my spirit upon all flesh; and your sons and your daughters shall prophesy, your old men shall dream dreams, your young men shall see visions:

29 And also upon the servants and upon the handmaids in those days will I pour out my spirit.

30 And I will shew wonders in the heavens and in the earth, blood, and fire, and pillars of smoke.

31 The sun shall be turned into darkness, and the moon into blood, before the great and the terrible day of the Lord come.

32 And it shall come to pass, that whosoever shall call on the name of the Lord shall be delivered: for in mount Zion and in Jerusalem shall be deliverance, as the Lord hath said, and in the remnant whom the Lord shall call.

So what was the first "get saved" message preached in the New Testament and where was it preached? Acts 2:38, 8:12-17, 10:40-48, 19:1-6. Hebrews 9:16:

16 For where a testament is, there must also of necessity be the death of the testator.

In order for a testament or will to be put into force, it requires the death of the one that instituted it. A last will and testament is not in force if the person is on life support. Only when they die does it come into force. The same is true with the new covenant or New Testament of God's will. The four gospels are a synopsis of the life of Christ. But the New Testament Church and salvation did not occur until His death and resurrection. The thief on the cross, whom Jesus spoke of paradise, was saved under the Old Testament covenant, because the Old Testament salvation plan stated one bring the correct sacrifice to the High Priest and confess their sin. Jesus was the sacrifice and the High Priest so He fulfilled the Old Testament requirements the thief was saved under.

Upon the day of Pentecost, the new will was put into force. This left many Believers in different places of progression concerning salvation. There were followers of John the Baptist, who were baptized unto repentance, believing on the Messiah to come. Their baptism was no longer valid after the day of Pentecost, because now water baptism is unto remission of sins. This is why Paul asked the baptist Believers in Acts 19:1-6, if they had been born of the spirit since they believed. When they said no, Paul asked how they were baptized? If you have not yet received the baptism of the spirit with the evidence of speaking in other tongues, my question is, how were you baptized? Paul re-baptized these followers into the name of Jesus Christ because **Acts 4:12** tells us:

12 Neither is there salvation in any other: for there is none other name under heaven given among men, whereby we must be saved.

Father, Son and Holy Ghost are not names, but positions of relationship.

Colossians 3:17

17 And whatsoever ye do in word or deed, do all in the name of the Lord Jesus, giving thanks to God and the Father by him.

Ephesians 3:15

15 Of whom the whole family in heaven and earth is named,

1 Corinthians 3:11

11 For other foundation can no man lay than that is laid, which is Jesus Christ.

Jesus Christ is the only foundation, which is why the apostle Paul re-baptized the baptist Believers into the name of Jesus Christ. When they obeyed this command to repent and be baptized in the name of Jesus Christ for the remission of sins, they fulfilled the first part of the covenant, and when they did this, God fulfilled His part of the covenant and filled them with His spirit with the evidence of speaking in other tongues. This was by the hand of the apostle Paul who also wrote the epistle to the Romans.

Many denominations try to establish a salvation, or a "get saved" message from the Book of Romans. But Romans 1:7 clearly states that this letter was written unto a Church who had already obeyed the "get saved" message. Should we assume that Paul preached two different gospels; one to the baptists Believers of Acts 19 and then a different "get saved" message to the group of Rome?

Paul emphatically states in **Galatians 1:6-9**:

6 I marvel that ye are so soon removed from him that called you into the grace of Christ unto another gospel:

7 Which is not another; but there be some that trouble you, and would pervert the gospel of Christ.

8 But though we, or an angel from heaven, preach any other gospel unto you than that which we have preached unto you, let him be accursed.

9 As we said before, so say I now again, If any man preach any other gospel unto you than that ye have received, let him be accursed.

Paul says that though he himself, or an angel from heaven would preach any different gospel, that he should be accursed. I think it is safe to assume that the apostle Paul preached the same initial plan of salvation, the same "get saved" message that Peter preached, because we find this out also from Galatians 1:17-18 and Galatians 2:1-2, which tells us that Paul checked his message with Peter.

Paul mentions "the gospel" in Romans 1:1, 9, 16, 2:16, 10:16, 11:28, 15:16, 29, and 16:25. Romans is Paul's defense of the gospel and is complete and sufficient for salvation, without keeping Old Testament circumcision. He needed to do this because there were two factions in the early Church in Rome. First there was the Jewish Christians, see Romans 2:23-29, who were declaring to the Gentile Believers the need for circumcision. This was a common problem in the early Church.

The Book of Galatians is also written against "Judaizers" and the whole subject is finally addressed and resolved in Acts 15. Romans 8:1 says there is now no condemnation to those who are in Christ Jesus. This would be pointless to write unless some Christians were condemning others as being insufficient. Paul concludes the Book of Romans in 16:17 by saying mark those who cause divisions and offenses contrary to the "doctrine" which you "have learned" (past tense).

Paul in Acts 19 preaches the same message as the apostle Peter in Acts 2:38, 10:38-48. Acts 8:12, 14-17 tells us when Phillip preached the gospel to Samaria, they were baptized into the name of the Lord Jesus Christ. These folks were repentant, they were Believers, they obeyed Phillip's preaching, and yet the spirit had not yet fallen on them according to verses 15 and 16. Many denominations preach that you automatically receive the spirit when you are baptized. That was not true in these scriptures now, was it? The gospel is the escape plan from all that shall come to pass in the end time, and every denomination preaches a different "get saved" message, saying that they are using the Bible, yet few preach the original message in the Book of Acts. Could this be our people in Matthew 7 who said they were Believers, but the Lord denied knowing them?

In Acts 10:40-48, Cornelius and the Romans received the spirit first and then were baptized. In Acts 11:15-18, Peter said that God gave the Gentiles the Holy Ghost just the same as He did to them in the beginning. In other words, the exact way. Again the apostle Peter, in Acts 15:7-9 states that God made a choice that the Gentiles would hear the gospel by the mouth of Peter and believe. And God who knows their hearts gave them the Holy Ghost in the exact way as they received it on the day of Pentecost, putting no difference between the apostles and the Gentile Believers. Please note in Romans 6:3-4, the apostle Paul mentions being baptized into Christ. Also note in Colossians 2:11-14, Paul calls water baptism the circumcision of Christ and that we are buried with Him. No where is the trinitarian formula, Father, Son and Holy Ghost, ever spoken over a baptismal candidate.

In Acts 18:24-26 we learn of a man named Apollos. It states he was eloquent in the scriptures, instructed in the Lord, knowing only the baptism of John. This man had a lot going for him, all pluses, nothing negative or anything bad to say about the man. He was, however, missing important ingredients: he was only baptized unto John's baptism. He needed water baptism in Jesus name and infilling of the Holy Ghost to be complete. So a husband and wife team, Aquilla and Priscilla, pulled him aside and gave him the rest of the story. Many of my denominational friends are good people. They are eloquent, learned people. Many are even mighty in the scriptures, living the lives of repentant Believers. We find several of those kind of people in the Book of Acts. Cornelius in Acts 10:1-4, was a devout man, a believer, a giver, one that prayed to God always. Many churches today would call

Cornelius saved, and yet an angel said to call for Peter because there was something he needed to do. When the apostle Paul spoke to the Believers of John the Baptist, there was not one negative thing to say about these folks. They were good people, godly people, repentant Believers, living lives for the Lord. However, they were not yet born again which is what Paul addressed.

My question to you, reader friend, are you a repentant believer? Do you study the word? Have you devoted your life to live for God? If so, then do you have the rest of the story? Like the apostle Paul, my question is, have you received the Holy Ghost and spoken in tongues since you believed? How were you baptized? Father, Son and Holy Ghost are titles and if we read Matthew 28:19, that scripture states there is one name, not names. It is the name that remits sin. Colossians 2:8 warns us to beware of traditions of men, and rudiments of this world, and not being totally after Christ. For, by the way, Paul said, in Christ dwells all the fullness of the godhead bodily. Paul was accosted in his religious duties by the Lord in Acts 9. Paul in Acts 9:5 said, "Who art thou Lord?" Here is the opportunity for divine revelation. Did the voice say, "We are Father, Son and Holy Ghost, the holy community"? Did the voice say, "We are the plurality of God"? Did the voice say, "I am the second person of the trinity"? It did not! It answered, "I am Jesus, whom you persecute." This is why Paul writes in 1 Corinthians 3:11 that the foundation is Jesus Christ, not trinity. This is why Paul says in Colossians 2:8-10 that the fullness of the godhead, the complete essence of all that God is, dwelt in Jesus Christ bodily, and we are complete in Him who is the head of all principality and power. This is why Jesus told Phillip, in John 14:8-10, "If you have seen Me, you have seen the Father. Have I been so long time with you and still you do not know Me, Phillip?" When Jesus made the statement in John 4:22, giving credence to the Jews religion, what was it the Jews knew about God?

Look at the Old Testament appearances of God in KJV Genesis 18:1-2, 22, 33, 19:1. There were three beings that appeared to Abraham. We find one of them, singular, was God. Other two were angels that went to Sodom. In Genesis 32:24-30, a being wrestled with Jacob. Yet in verse 30, Jacob said, "I have seen God face to face." The man that wrestled with him was God Himself. In Exodus 24:10-11, 33:9-11, Moses brought Israel out of Egypt, and they all saw a vision of God as a towering immense single being. In Isaiah 6:1-6, we again encounter three beings. One Lord on one throne, and two six-winged seraphim. In Ezekiel 1:26-28, he has a vision of God, and there is a man on a throne. In Joshua 5:15, he is confronted with the captain of the Lord's hosts. But chapter 6:2 says, "The LORD said unto Joshua..." Again, a singular being. God said in Deuteronomy 6:4, "Hear, O Israel, the Lord our God is one." Someone is right and someone is wrong. The trinity doctrine says Father, Son and Holy Ghost are actually three coequal, coeternal, individuals. However, all through the Old Testament He emphatically declared that He was one, every appearance He made, He was a singular being. If trinity is correct, God was deliberately deceptive before He got to the New Testament, or, a plurality of persons is an addition to scripture that was not originally there. Study Constantine and Nicea 325 A.D.

Could the trinity doctrine be the three measures of meal Jesus spoke of a woman adding in Matthew 13:33? Could this be why God is so viciously angry at the woman in Revelation 17? Is it possible that those who will not submit to the apostles' gospel in the Book of Acts to repent of their sins, to be water baptized by immersion in the name of Jesus Christ for the remission of sins and receive His spirit with the evidence of speaking in other tongues, are those people who will be the confused Believers in Matthew 7:22? Is this why Jesus said, "I never knew you" because they preached a godhead that does not exist? Scripture does mention a Father, Son and Holy Ghost. These are Biblical terms. But terms commonly mentioned in the Trinitarian doctrine that are not Biblical are: God the Son, eternally begotten Son of God, God the Holy Ghost. Father, Son and Hloy Ghost, Holy Spirit, Spirit of Christ, Spirit of God all are terms speaking of how God relates to man.

If the escape ticket from the coming wrath is obedience to the apostles' gospel message, why in the world would we hesitate to obey it exactly as they originally preached it? If you are a minister, and have read the Book of Acts, you surely know, as the apostles said, in Hebrews 13:17, "the ministry must give an account at the throne for the souls they ministered to." Which board do you fear the most? The denomination, or the heavenly board?

It is not my intention to offend, but to inform and to move you to search out the original gospel message the apostles' preached in the Book of Acts. Epistles are letters written to established Churches. They do not present an initial "get saved" message, but a stay saved message. If there is a "church" they became "church" by obeying the gospel. Paul spoke to the Church in Rome and, in Romans 8:15-16, Paul tells the Church in Rome that they have already received the spirit. Romans 6:17, says they have obeyed, past tense, the form of doctrine that was delivered unto them. Romans 16:16-18 tells us that the Churches of Christ salute them. It says to mark those that cause division contrary to the doctrine they have learned (past tense). Since Paul is the author of Romans, go to Acts 19:1-6, and see what Paul's "get saved" message is. We must be careful that we have the Bible truth and that our definitions fit Bible definitions.

Many people receive a supernatural experience, but then, interpret that through their own opinion. For example, we knew a man once who was crippled and prayed continually that God would help him walk. He received a partial healing with a witness of a glory cloud in his room. He then attached his own interpretation and told me, "now I know I am saved", basing it on this experience with God. Many people say, "I believe in Jesus Christ. Therefore I am saved." Sound rules of Biblical interpretation require that you take all the scriptures that speak on the subject, put them together, and see what they collectively say. Also, it is important to look up the Greek or Hebrew meaning of the original words. Using a Strong's Exhaustive Concordance of the Bible and a Thayer's Greek English Lexicon of the New Testament will aid in your Biblical study and research.

DENNIS & LINDA KROG

CHAPTER 7
THE SEALS

In Revelation, chapter 6, we see the Lamb begins to open a book sealed with seven seals. The seals contain the announcements of the intended, predetermined wrath of God, which reveal God's plan. The blowing of each trumpet by the angel announces that this judgment is coming, and when the vial is poured out, the judgment begins. The seal reveals what the judgment will be, the trumpet announces that judgment, and the vial is the actual action of the judgment. "Tribulation" is used in this book to refer to the seven year period. "Great Tribulation" refers to the last 3 ½ years of the seven years after the peace plan from the antichrist is broken.

The wrath of God is something that is prophesied all through the Bible.

Nahum 1:2

2 God is jealous, and the Lord revengeth; the Lord revengeth, and is furious; the Lord will take vengeance on his adversaries, and he reserveth wrath for his enemies.

Zephaniah 1:14-18

14 The great day of the Lord is near, it is near, and hasteth greatly, even the voice of the day of the Lord: the mighty man shall cry there bitterly.

15 That day is a day of wrath, a day of trouble and distress, a day of wasteness and desolation, a day of darkness and gloominess, a day of clouds and thick darkness,

16 A day of the trumpet and alarm against the fenced cities, and against the high towers.

17 And I will bring distress upon men, that they shall walk like blind men, because they have sinned against the Lord: and their blood shall be poured out as dust, and their flesh as the dung.

18 Neither their silver nor their gold shall be able to deliver them in the day of the Lord's wrath; but the whole land shall be devoured by the fire of his jealousy: for he shall make even a speedy riddance of all them that dwell in the land.

Joel 2:31-32

31 The sun shall be turned into darkness, and the moon into blood, before the great and the terrible day of the Lord come.

32 And it shall come to pass, that whosoever shall call on the name of the Lord shall be delivered: for in mount Zion and in Jerusalem shall be deliverance, as the Lord hath said, and in the remnant whom the Lord shall call.

Psalms 110:5-6

5 The Lord at thy right hand shall strike through kings in the day of his wrath.

6 He shall judge among the heathen, he shall fill the places with the dead bodies; he shall wound the heads over many countries.

Ezekiel 7:19

19 They shall cast their silver in the streets, and their gold shall be removed: their silver and their gold shall not be able to deliver them in the day of the wrath of the Lord: they shall not satisfy their souls, neither fill their bowels: because it is the stumblingblock of their iniquity.

Isaiah 66:14-18

14 And when ye see this, your heart shall rejoice, and your bones shall flourish like an herb: and the hand of the Lord shall be known toward his servants, and his indignation toward his enemies.

15 For, behold, the Lord will come with fire, and with his chariots like a whirlwind, to render his anger with fury, and his rebuke with flames of fire.

16 For by fire and by his sword will the Lord plead with all flesh: and the slain of the Lord shall be many.

17 They that sanctify themselves, and purify themselves in the gardens behind one tree in the midst, eating swine's flesh, and the abomination, and the mouse, shall be consumed together, saith the Lord.

18 For I know their works and their thoughts: it shall come, that I will gather all nations and tongues; and they shall come, and see my glory.

Matthew 3:7

7 But when he saw many of the Pharisees and Sadducees come to his baptism, he said unto them, O generation of vipers, who hath warned you to flee from the wrath to come?

Romans 1:18

18 For the wrath of God is revealed from heaven against all ungodliness and unrighteousness of men, who hold the truth in unrighteousness;

Romans 1:32

32 Who knowing the judgment of God, that they which commit such things are worthy of death, not only do the same, but have pleasure in them that do them.

Romans 2:5-10

5 But after thy hardness and impenitent heart treasurest up unto thyself wrath against the day of wrath and revelation of the righteous judgment of God;

6 Who will render to every man according to his deeds:

7 To them who by patient continuance in well doing seek for glory and honour and immortality, eternal life:

8 But unto them that are contentious, and do not obey the truth, but obey unrighteousness, indignation and wrath,

9 Tribulation and anguish, upon every soul of man that doeth evil, of the Jew first, and also of the Gentile;

10 But glory, honour, and peace, to every man that worketh good, to the Jew first, and also to the Gentile:

Romans 9:22-24

22 What if God, choosing to show his wrath and make his power known, bore with great patience the objects of his wrath — prepared for destruction? 23 What if he did this to make the riches of his glory known to the objects of his mercy, whom he prepared in advance for glory— 24 even us, whom he also called, not only from the Jews but also from the Gentiles?

The former scriptures collectively tell us that right from the ancient times, the entire scope of man's existence on earth has been planned out by God from beginning to end. There has been a warning from day one that there will be wrath upon the disobedient. But there are also scriptures that say that those who seek mercy and obey the Truth with diligence and caution concerning the Word of God, will be spared from wrath. In Matthew 5:9, 1 Thessalonians 1:10 and 5:9 we read we shall be spared from wrath if we have obeyed the gospel. Such scriptures as Romans 2:8, 2 Thessalonians 1:8, 1 Peter 4:17, Romans 6:17, Romans 10:16, 1 Peter 1:22 all talk about obeying "the Truth" and obeying "the gospel" so that we are delivered from the wrath to come. Since the apostle Paul said that the Church shall be delivered from wrath, and the breaking of the seals is the revealing of the wrath of God, and since the word "Church" is not mentioned after chapter 4 in Revelation, and since there is a multitude in heaven in chapter 5, we can conclude the Church has been raptured into heaven prior to chapter 6, which is the beginning of the 70th week of Daniel for the Jewish people spoken of in Daniel 9:24.

Now we will discuss the seals. Upon opening the first seal, there is a rider on a white horse. He has a bow, but no arrows. He has a crown which tells us he is a ruler. He went forth conquering and to conquer. In this case the white horse and bow without arrows is a symbol of conquering through peace. We refer to Daniel 8:23-25 in which we are told that in the latter time of the Gentile kingdoms, when the transgressors are come to the full, a king of fierce countenance will arise, and it says by peace shall destroy many. This statement tells us that the entire world are of one mind, because the transgressors are come to the full, or fully made their decision against God. Once again, there is no "Left Behind" because the transgressors are come to the full. This is why God is pouring out His wrath on Gentile nations. The only people to be saved after this are Jews and those who become Jews, and those who will live to see the Millennial Reign, which are indeed few. There are those who have chosen to obey the gospel, they are the Church – they are with Christ. Then there are those who are merely religious and are deceived, not diligently seeking the truth of how to be born again. Jesus referred to them as workers of iniquity in Matthew 7:21, because they did not obey His words. And the third group is the unpurified Jewish nation. These two and the Gentile nations are left for the antichrist to rule.

The second seal announces a rider on a red horse who brings in war and bloodshed. NOTE: the same rider has now switched horses. The rider on all of the horses is the antichrist.

The third seal announces a black horse and the rider has a pair of balances. Black is worn by judges and balances are used to transact business. This is a picture telling us that war is costly, therefore, he is seeking to use the world's wealth of which he will now be in full control. In verse 6 the word announces a measure of wheat for a penny, and a measure of barley for a penny, and see that you hurt not the wine and the oil. At the time of the King James translation, a penny was a day's wage. Therefore, this is telling us it will be so bad that a loaf of bread or a bagel will cost a day's wage. The wine and oil, however, belong to the rich and the antichrist does not want them harmed as he plans to use their resources.

The fourth seal is in chapter 6:8 and reveals a pale horse. Disease quite often follows war and death. Many unburied bodies breed disease. Here, one fourth of the population of the world dies. When one considers between 6 and 7 billion people on the planet, what is ¼ of that? Close to 3 billion people that die suddenly from war and disease because the Bible talks about "power was given over the fourth part of the earth to kill with the sword, with hunger, with death and wild beasts."

The fifth seal (verse 9) reveals Jews that are slain for their testimony of the Word of God. These are Jews by heredity and there are Jews that practice the religion seeking a true connection with God. The slain are those Jews who have stood against the antichrist and kept their faith in God. Verse 11 mentions "their brethren". These are Jews also, and in the remainder of this book, the term "saints" or "brethren" refers to the faithful Jewish people remaining on the earth.

The sixth seal (verse 12) is broken, fulfilling the prophecy of Joel 2:31 telling us that the sun becomes black, the moon becomes as blood, possibly an eclipse or a "blood moon." The next verse says the stars fall to the earth in a great number, like a fig tree casting its figs when shaken of the wind. Verse 14 talks about the heavens departing and every mountain departing out of their places. This obviously will cause worldwide devastation and terror as well as total destruction. Verse 15 – 17 describe the great fear of the kings, the great men, the rich men, and the military, all running to rocks and caves to hide themselves because they see the face of Him (not them) who sets on the throne.   What chapter 6 has contained for us is a panorama, or a snapshot of what will be spoken hereafter. This same idea has been used before in the Book of Genesis where chapter 1 gives an overall picture of creation and chapter 2 goes into more detail.

The sealing of the servants of God is found in Revelation 7:4-8. These mention the tribes of Israel, excluding Dan. Verses 9-16 mention a great multitude, now before the throne of God. Verse 14 tells us they came out of Great Tribulation (the last 3 ½ years) and have washed their robes in the blood of the Lamb, which is obtained through water baptism in Jesus name. The Bible states emphatically that the gospel is an everlasting gospel and Jesus is the Lamb of God

(Revelation 14:6). Therefore, the same gospel to save the Gentile Church today will be the same gospel to save the Jewish faithful during the Tribulation. Verse 7:17 tells us that He shall lead them unto living fountains of waters and God shall wipe all tears from their eyes. Living fountains of waters refers to the birth of the spirit, as spoken of in John 7:37-39 speaking of living water being the spirit of Jesus Christ, or the Holy Ghost, which Believers should receive. See also KJV Psalm 46:4, Isaiah 12:1-6, Isaiah 55:1. Since the Church that has obeyed the gospel has already been baptized in Jesus name and has already received the baptism of the Holy Ghost with the evidence of speaking in other tongues (Isaiah 28:11-12, Joel 2:28, John 3:8, Mark 16:16, Acts 2:4, Acts 2:38, Acts 10:46-47, Acts 19:5-6), obviously this multitude in heaven in Revelation 7 is not talking about the Church, but Jews who have come to the revelation that Jesus Christ is the Messiah and have begun to obey the everlasting gospel by being baptized in Jesus name, and Jesus gives them the living water, which they have not yet received. The end of verse 17 tells us that all tears will be wiped from their eyes because they came out of Great Tribulation of which the apostle Paul said, the Church was spared. Chapter 6 was the beginning of Daniel's 70th week. We turn your attention to **Romans 11:25-27**:

25 For I would not, brethren, that ye should be ignorant of this mystery, lest ye should be wise in your own conceits; that blindness in part is happened to Israel, until the fulness of the Gentiles be come in.

26 And so all Israel shall be saved: as it is written, There shall come out of Sion the Deliverer, and shall turn away ungodliness from Jacob:

27 For this is my covenant unto them, when I shall take away their sins.

So, these scriptures are telling us that Israel's blindness will not be removed until the Gentile Church is complete. Then, what is left of Israel shall be saved.

Micah 5:3

3 Therefore will he give them up, until the time that she which travaileth hath brought forth: then the remnant of his brethren shall return unto the children of Israel.

The word "fullness" in Romans 11:25 is the number 4138 in Strong's and Thayer's. The word means "full number". So then, after the full number of the Gentiles are come in, no more can be added to the full number. Micah also says that God will give up Israel until she which travails has brought forth. This is a word picture of the Gentile Church, which intercedes in prayer and worship. Now when the full number has been accomplished and the Church has been removed from the wrath to come, His attention is fully turned to the redeeming of Israel. The afore mentioned prophecy in Daniel 9:24 told us of the one remaining seven year period to make an end of transgressions, to anoint the most Holy, to bring in everlasting righteousness. This is now being fulfilled in the time period in Revelation chapter 6 and after. To this we also add 2 Thessalonians 2:6-13:

THE FINAL STORY

6 And now ye know what withholdeth that he might be revealed in his time.

The "what withholdeth" means the One that restrains, which is the Holy Ghost power in the Church. "That he might be revealed in his time" is the antichrist who shall be revealed in God's time.

7 For the mystery of iniquity doth already work: only he who now letteth will let, until he be taken out of the way.

"He who now letteth" means there is One who restrains. Again we are talking about the Holy Ghost. "Until he be taken out of the way". It is important that the Holy Ghost in the Church be taken out of the way because the antichrist is a satan possessed man and there are multitudes of scripture references giving the Church authority and power over demons (Mark 16:17, 1 John 4:4, Luke 10:19, Matthew 10:1, 8, Mark 3:15). Since these verses are always true, we see the Church with authority over demons must be removed for the demonic presence to take authority in this earth.

8 And then shall that Wicked be revealed, whom the Lord shall consume with the spirit of his mouth, and shall destroy with the brightness of his coming:

9 Even him, whose coming is after the working of Satan with all power and signs and lying wonders,

10 And with all deceivableness of unrighteousness in them that perish; because they received not the love of the truth, that they might be saved.

11 And for this cause God shall send them strong delusion, that they should believe a lie:

12 That they all might be damned who believed not the truth, but had pleasure in unrighteousness.

Verses 11 and 12 tells us there is no further Gentiles to be saved because God Himself will send deceiving angels that those left on the earth might all believe a lie because they did not receive a love of "the Truth".

13 But we are bound to give thanks alway to God for you, brethren beloved of the Lord, because God hath from the beginning chosen you to salvation through sanctification of the Spirit and belief of the truth:

14 Whereunto he called you by our gospel, to the obtaining of the glory of our Lord Jesus Christ.

The seventh seal is opened in Revelation chapter 8:1, announcing all of the final judgments. Now that all the seals are open, and the judgments are known to John, now in Revelation 8:6, what happens at the blowing of the seven trumpets is revealed to John, so John can see, in further detail, what occurs when the seals are opened in a gruesome play by play report. We will skip ahead now to chapter 10:1-4, where we see a mighty angel that, when he cries, seven thunders utter their voices. It was revealed to John what they said, and as he was about to write, a voice from heaven said, "Seal up those things which the seven thunders uttered and write them not." One must wonder what John knew, and this world will no doubt tremble greatly when it is finally revealed.

CHAPTER 8
THE WOMAN

Revelation chapter 11 talks about the Temple of God and those who worship therein for 42 months, or 3 ½ years. There are two witnesses introduced in 11:3. Some speculate that one of these will be John himself, because Revelation 10:11 states, "thou must prophesy again before many peoples and nations and tongues and kings." According to history, John did not do any of that after he recorded Revelation. So we can conclude he has not yet fulfilled that prophecy about his life. Indeed, there was a theory that circulated among Jesus' disciples that John would never die (John 21:20-23). In Revelation 11:4, there are two witnesses that are two olive trees and two candlesticks standing before the God of the earth. One wonders if the first of these witnesses is either Moses or Elijah. Possibly Elijah because he never died but was taken to heaven in a fiery chariot (2 Kings 2:11). Since Elijah was the Old Testament prophet who worked miracles and withstood evil kings to bring Israel to repentance, and John is the New Testament prophet writing the prophecy of Revelation, these would be representative of the two covenants, old and new.

In chapter 12 of Revelation, verse 1-6, Israel is described in picture language. She is described as a woman, clothed with the sun, having the moon under her feet and a crown of 12 stars on her head. The stars are the 12 tribes of Israel, the sun is the glory of God, the moon under her feet represents the Church that she is also mother of, who has no glory of its own but reflects the glory and light of the Son of God. This woman was in pain to be delivered of a child, which was the Messiah. Verse 3 talks about a great red dragon, having seven heads with seven crowns and ten horns. This is the devil, and that of the beast, which is a governmental system and its rulers, later discussed in chapter 13. Verse 4 tells how the dragon did throw a third part of the stars to the earth. It is known that 1/3 of the angelic host fell with satan when he was cast out of heaven. Those former angels are now demons. The dragon tried to kill and devour the child through Herod who slaughtered all the children from two years old and under at the time of Jesus' childhood. Verse 5 tells us that the child was caught up to God and His throne. This is the child prophesied to come in **Isaiah 7:14** and 9:6.

14 Therefore the Lord himself shall give you a sign; Behold, a virgin shall conceive, and bear a son, and shall call his name Immanuel.

Isaiah 9:6

6 For unto us a child is born, unto us a son is given: and the government shall be upon his shoulder: and his name shall be called Wonderful, Counsellor, The mighty God, The everlasting Father, The Prince of Peace.

Verse 9 of Revelation 12 also mentions that the devil and his angels were cast out, further agreeing with verse 4. In verse 14, the woman was given two wings of a great eagle that she might fly into the wilderness. This is speaking of God's deliverance and not alluding to any country of man. In Exodus 19:4, when God delivered Israel from Egypt, He said, "I bear you on eagle's wings." (See also Psalm 91:4) The Bible says, the earth helped the woman and opened her mouth and swallowed the flood that the dragon cast out of his mouth. What this actually will look like, the Bible does not conjecture and neither will we. Some things in Revelation will not be known and understood until the day it happens. However, the remnant of Israel will God hide away and protect to reign in the earthly Jerusalem during the Millennium.

DENNIS & LINDA KROG

CHAPTER 9
ONE WORLD GOVERNMENTAL SYSTEM

In Revelation 13:1, John sees a beast rise up out of the sea, having seven heads and ten horns and ten crowns upon the horns. This is the same beast seen by Daniel in chapter 7:2-7 of that book, corresponding to Nebuchadnezzar's image. The seven heads are:

1. Egypt
2. Assyria
3. Babylon (Nebuchadnezzar's image began here)
4. Medio-Persia
5. Greece
6. Rome
7. Antichrist kingdom (iron and clay mixed). His kingdom will arise out of the former Roman Empire nations.

The ten horns correspond to the ten toes which equal the ten kingdoms and their rulers of the antichrist final kingdom. Again, this has been conjectured as possibly being the ECM (European Common Market). Verse 2 says that the dragon gave this "beast" his power and his authority. Verse 3 says one head appears to be wounded to death, but the deadly wound becomes healed and all the world wonders about the beast. The deadly wound corresponds to Rome which suffered its demise around 476 B.C. This entire beast represents one world dictator rule. The Caesars were the last of the one world dictators. That form of government received a deadly wound, but never completely died. The spirit has been kept alive through the institution of a Roman emperor named Constantine. We will discuss this further in Revelation 17.

Is it possible that this ten nation alliance of the end time could be the godless European Common Market, which today have bound themselves together, and have established a singular currency which most of them accept, and are merely waiting for their leader? In 1996, Linda and her parents traveled through Germany to Norway to visit relations. After purchasing souvenirs in Norway, the clerk told her Linda would need to pay duty on the items when she left the country. Linda said they would be exiting in Oslo. The woman just stared at her and paused. Then said, no, when you leave "the Country." She asked where Linda would fly out of to return to the USA? Linda said Germany.

The woman explained all the nations are called "The Country," also known as the EU – European Union. They are all one country and act like the United States, in that trade within is free. Interesting. The beast is further spoken of in Revelation 17:10 which says there are seven kings. Five are fallen at the time of John's writing, one is, which was Rome, and the other is not yet come, which is the final kingdom of the antichrist.

Chapter 13:16 mentions the antichrist causes all that dwell on the earth to receive a mark (most likely a computer microchip), in their right hand or in their forehead, that no one could buy or sell without the mark. Chapter 14:9 and 10 tells us if any receive the mark, they are damned. Revelation at this point has not been in chronological order since chapter 5. So the mark probably is instituted at the beginning of the seven year Tribulation. Chapter 15 tells of the last seven plagues in the form of vials. Verse 3 tells of a multitude that sings the song of Moses and the Lamb. These would be Messianic Jews converted during the Tribulation. In verse 15:7, we are told the seven angels are given seven vials full of the wrath of God. The seals were broken, the trumpets have heralded the event, and now it is happening. John, now, is witnessing what the vials in succession cause to occur. The battle of Armageddon, the final war, and is mentioned in verses 14-16.

Chapter 17, 18 and 19 talk about the destruction of the lady in red, also called "the Great Whore" and "Mystery Babylon." In order to facilitate understanding we will establish references to her as "the Lady in Red" (17:1). We are also told that the "Lady in Red" sits upon many waters, referring to 17:15 which are peoples, multitudes, nations and languages.

Verse 17:2 tells us that the kings of the earth have been made drunk with the wine of her fornication. Popes and Cardinals crowned kings and also threatened them with excommunication. In the Old Testament, when Israel served idolatry and false gods, God called her an Adulteress (see Jeremiah 3:8, 5:7, Ezekiel 23:36-37, Hosea 1:2). Bear in mind, "a woman" in prophecy either speaks of Israel or a Church. Chapter 17:3 of Revelation says she rides upon a scarlet colored beast, which is the end time kingdom. Verse 4 describes the woman arrayed in purple and scarlet. Bishops wore purple and Cardinals wore red. We are told that in her hand is a golden cup full of abomination and filthiness of her fornication. This is her doctrine of the Lord's supper, i.e. transubstantiation, and that every mass Christ is again crucified and offered up. Rather than proclaiming the apostles' new birth gospel of water baptism in Jesus name for a repentant believer and infilling of the Holy Ghost with the evidence of speaking in tongues, she proclaims that forgiveness of sins and the life of Christ are imparted through taking of the Lord's supper as they teach it. This Church was inaugurated by a pagan Roman Emperor named Constantine, who called together the bishops of Churches in 325 A.D. to the city of Nicea. Approximately 1/6 of them showed up, most of them refusing to come to a religious council led by an unbaptized heathen leader. In this council, Constantine gave forth his opinion and wrote into political law what was established during that council. In 381, the council of Constantinople I finalized the Nicene Creed and established that the Holy Ghost was a separate and distinct third person. There were seven ecumenical councils, each of which anathematized and excommunicated people who disagreed with them, many times being reinstated at a later council. At all seven of the councils, the question came up, who is Jesus? Was He of the same substance as the Father? Was He a separate and distinct other substance? Was He an appointed being? Because, by 325 A.D., so much Greek mythology and philosophy had crept into some of the Christian doctrine, that the baptism of the Holy Ghost no longer generally fell on Believers, and they did not even know for sure who Jesus was. They had lost the revelation by allowing pagan beliefs into the doctrine. They now baptized unbelieving, unrepentant infants as well as codifying conversion or making it a law to convert, or be killed. There was no true conversion experience with God in the lives of those growing up in this church, to be a pagan or to believe anything other than what this political monster taught meant being burned the stake. The Word of God, originally written in Greek, which was the common language of the world in its day, was now translated into Latin, a dead language, which the common man did not know. This plunged the world into the "Dark Ages" by taking away the Bible and sealing it up where only a few could read it and interpret its meaning to their own ends. This Church claims Peter to be its first pope. If this is so, then why do they not preach the first salvation message that Peter preached in Acts 2:38 and Acts 10:38-48? Hmmmm....

We will return now to **Revelation 17:6**.

6 And I saw the woman drunken with the blood of the saints, and with the blood of the martyrs of Jesus: and when I saw her, I wondered with great admiration.

This verse is describing those that this Church slaughtered by burning at the stake anyone they considered a heretic, by the Inquisition and Holy Wars. One only needs to ask, did Jesus and His disciples kill anyone because of religious fervor? James and John asked Jesus if they should call down fire, and Jesus said, "You know not what spirit you are of because the son of man is not come to destroy men's lives, but to save them." (Luke 9:54-56) How did they reach this point of apostacy?

In **Revelation 17:7-8**, the angel tells John,

7 And the angel said unto me, Wherefore didst thou marvel? I will tell thee the mystery of the woman, and of the beast that carrieth her, which hath the seven heads and ten horns.

8 The beast that thou sawest was, and is not; and shall ascend out of the bottomless pit, and go into perdition: and they that dwell on the earth shall wonder, whose names were not written in the book of life from the foundation of the world, when they behold the beast that was, and is not, and yet is.

John is seeing a government at a future time. Please notice those left are not written in the Book of Life. It is said that the Beast was, and is not, and yet is. It ceased to be in the period of the Roman Empire, and yet it is revived in the antichrist kingdom. The "it" is one world dictatorship rule that ceased with the Roman Empire.

Let us look further in verses 9 and 10:

9 And here is the mind which hath wisdom. The seven heads are seven mountains, on which the woman sitteth.

10 And there are seven kings: five are fallen, and one is, and the other is not yet come; and when he cometh, he must continue a short space.

The seven heads are seven mountains. There is only one great city in the world that is known to set on seven hills – that is Rome, which is further confirmed in verse 18 which says the woman is a great city and reigns over kings of the earth. As we stated before, Popes and cardinals crowned kings. Verse 10 tells us of the seven kings, of which five are fallen. These would be the kings of Egypt, Assyria, Babylon, Medio-Persia, and Greece. Verse 10 says the one is – that is Rome (at the time John saw the vision). The other is not yet come, which is the antichrist kingdom. Verse 12 tells us, the ten horns are ten kings. Verse 13 says they will in unity give their power and strength to the beast, or governmental system. The King of kings will return to make war with this final kingdom (Revelation 17:14). Note, they that are with Him are called, chosen and faithful. These are the people that had left prior to the Tribulation to be with Him, the Church (Jude 14 and 15), and are now returning with Him.

Chapter 18 is a continuance of chapter 17. Verse 4 of chapter 18 issues a loving command from God that says,

4 And I heard another voice from heaven, saying, Come out of her, my people, that ye be not partakers of her sins, and that ye receive not of her plagues.

5 For her sins have reached unto heaven, and God hath remembered her iniquities.

From these two scriptures, we conclude that God cares very much about "His people." I know many sincere, devout, loving, caring, good people that belong to this religion. But God's words to this people are, "Come out of her." I would say the same loving invitation. Please read the Book of Acts, see what the apostle Peter preached and find a Church that preaches this message!

Rev 18:16-20

16 And saying, Alas, alas, that great city, that was clothed in fine linen, and purple, and scarlet, and decked with gold, and precious stones, and pearls!

17 For in one hour so great riches is come to nought. And every shipmaster, and all the company in ships, and sailors, and as many as

trade by sea, stood afar off,

18 And cried when they saw the smoke of her burning, saying, What city is like unto this great city!

19 And they cast dust on their heads, and cried, weeping and wailing, saying, Alas, alas, that great city, wherein were made rich all that had ships in the sea by reason of her costliness! for in one hour is she made desolate.

20 Rejoice over her, thou heaven, and ye holy apostles and prophets; for God hath avenged you on her.

We mentioned earlier the spirit of Roman dictatorship was kept alive by Constantine because in the formation of a religious Roman Catholic Church, the Pope became the supreme dictator of this new religion. He is worshipped as "Holy Father" and is said to be infallible. The description of this Lady in Red becomes quite obvious, but John was living 300 years before her existence. He only described what he saw in a vision. As we look at chapter 18:16, we see the Lady in Red is that great city. Fine linen, purple and scarlet, speak of the vestments of her various levels of ministry. Decked with gold, precious stones and pearls, indicate the lavish rings, garments and temples, along with its furnishings. When one looks at the Book of Acts to the first Church that met in homes, the ministers who were lucky to own a change of clothes, one must ask, how did we get here? These are the vestments of Emperors, and their palaces.

Chapter 18:17 speaks of the great riches and trade of this city.

As many know, the Vatican bank is the richest in all the earth. Her commerce includes land, ships, buildings, carved works of idols with gold overlay, great art works, as well as billions of dollars in interest from loans made from the Vatican bank to the world leaders and nations. God does not hate the people. What God is opposed to is any swerving from the Truth and "the gospel". Some other doctrines which are included in the Roman Catholic Church which are not found anywhere in the Bible are:

1. Prayers for the dead
2. Veneration of angels and dead "saints" that began approximately 375 A.D.
3. Worship of Mary, the mother of Jesus changed to the "Mother of God" originated in Council of Ephesus in 431 A.D. How could Mary be the mother of One who existed before the beginning of all creation?
4. Doctrine of Purgatory established by Pope Gregory the Great approximately A.D. 593.
5. Latin language instituted for prayer and worship by Pope Gregory I A.D. 610.
6. Title of "Pope" given to the Bishop in Rome A.D. 610.
7. Kissing of Pope's feet began A.D. 890.
8. Worship of the cross, images and relics authorized A.D. 788.
9. Holy water with a pinch of salt blessed by the priest authorized A.D. 850.

10. Canonization of dead "saints" began A.D. 995

11. Celibacy of the priesthood instituted by the popes Hildebrand and Boniface VII in A.D. 709 contrary to 1 Timothy 4:3.

12. The Rosary, or prayer beads instituted by Peter the Hermit in A.D. 1090, and was copied from the Hindus and Mohammedans.

13. The inquisition of heretics instituted by the Council of Verena in A.D. 1184.

14. Widespread sale of indulgences commonly regarded as a purchase of forgiveness for money was a permit to indulge in sin beginning in A.D. 1190.

15. The dogma of transubstantiation instituted by Pope Innocent II in A.D. 1215.

16. Obligatory confession of sins to a priest at least once per year instituted by Pope Innocent III at the Lateran Council in A.D. 1215.

17. The Bible forbidden to laymen and placed in the index of forbidden books by the Council at Valencia in A.D. 1229.

18. Forbidding of the communion cup to the laity meaning they were only offered the wafer, not the cup, instituted at the Council of Constance in A.D. 1414.

19. Doctrine of purgatory, now proclaimed a dogma of faith by the Council of Florence, A.D. 1439.

20. The doctrine of seven sacraments instituted A.D. 1439.

21. Council of Trent A.D. 1545 declared Church tradition equal to the

authority of the Bible.

22. Apocryphal books added to the Bible by the Council of Trent A.D. 1546.

23. Immaculate conception of virgin Mary, proclaimed by Pope Pius IX in A.D. 1854.

24. Pope Pius IX proclaimed the dogma of papal infallibility A.D. 1870.

25. Pope Pius X in A.D. 1907 condemned "modernism" and all discoveries of modern science that were not approved by the Roman Catholic Church.

26. Bodily assumption of Mary was made a dogma in A.D. 1950.

27. Mary proclaimed Queen Mother of Heaven, God, Christ and the Church, A.D. 1965.

28. Pope John Paul II declared forgiveness of sins can be obtained only through the Catholic Church A.D. 1985.

This is a partial list compiled by Rev. Lee Stoneking in the School of the Scriptures, page 135. It is enough to say that God fearing religious good people have been deceived and led astray by high ranking clerics and have not taught the necessary salvation message preached by the apostles. This is why the loving Saviour, with His people, issue a loving call, "Come out of her My people, that ye be not partakers of her sins" (Revelation 18:4). Can one be devout and yet incomplete? Can one be sincere and be sincerely wrong? Can one be religious and not saved? Can one read God's book and miss it? The answer to all of these questions is yes. The Bible says when the blind lead the blind, they both fall in the ditch (Matthew 15:14).

DENNIS & LINDA KROG

CHAPTER 10
GUESS WHO'S COMING TO JUDGMENT?

The same One who came to a stable and has been rejected of man ever since, is coming back on a white horse. This time he is coming as the undisputed conquering champion!

Rev 19:11-16

11 And I saw heaven opened, and behold a white horse; and he that sat upon him was called Faithful and True, and in righteousness he doth judge and make war.

12 His eyes were as a flame of fire, and on his head were many crowns; and he had a name written, that no man knew, but he himself.

13 And he was clothed with a vesture dipped in blood: and his name is called The Word of God.

14 And the armies which were in heaven followed him upon white horses, clothed in fine linen, white and clean.

15 And out of his mouth goeth a sharp sword, that with it he should smite the nations: and he shall rule them with a rod of iron: and he treadeth the winepress of the fierceness and wrath of Almighty God.

16 And he hath on his vesture and on his thigh a name written, KING OF KINGS, AND LORD OF LORDS.

Chapter 20:2 assures us satan will be bound for a thousand years, thus ushering in the millennial reign. Chapter 20:6 says the priests of God shall reign with Him a thousand years. At the end of this thousand year period, according the 20:7, satan is again loosed out of his prison. 20:8-10 says he again gathers nations to battle. Can you imagine, after 1000 years of glory, in a true Utopia, there will still be those who are just waiting for a chance to rebel!? To occasion a final sifting, God allows satan to call out to those who will hear his evil voice to come again to battle the reigning Messiah and His saints. Satan is immediately cast into the lake of fire which causes an end to this present world. This brings us to verses 11-15, the great White Throne judgment. The heavens and the earth flee away. Isaiah 34:1-6 which describes the heavens being rolled together as a scroll. Revelation 20:12 tells us all that have ever lived stand before the throne of God. The books with the accounts of their lives are opened. Another book is opened which is the Lamb's Book of Life and the people are judged by their works according to what is written in their life account. Revelation 20:14 says that death and hell, being like a county jail, are now cast in to the penitentiary of the Lake of Fire. Chapter 21 describes a new heaven and a new earth. Jesus Christ is the one sitting on the throne in verses 5-7. In chapter 22, Jesus issues a final invitation. Verses 12-17 tells us that Jesus Christ is God Almighty, and the Spirit and the Bride issue an invitation and say, "Come." To those who are thirsty, "Come". Do you want the water of life? "Come." We await you.

DENNIS & LINDA KROG

CHAPTER 11
SUMMARY

In conclusion, we see that God has been saying the same thing since He gave the law at Sinai through the Book of Revelation. God has a plan. History is in fact His story. Nothing is left to chance. The events are predestined, the salvation plan in the time of Genesis was Noah's Ark. The salvation plan for Lot was flee to the mountains. The salvation plan for the people of Israel was to receive the Law, obey it, and enter into the Promised Land. In the New Testament, to enter the Church, we leave Egypt, so to speak, we obey God's Word in the gospel, and enter into the Promised Land of Heaven.

The feasts of the Old Testament foretold the coming of the Messiah, the time of the Church age, the escape from judgment, the reconciliation of the nation of Israel, and the final 1000 year reign of Jerusalem. Then the White Throne judgment with a new heaven and new earth. Every period of judgment had a provision for deliverance of the righteous before the coming judgment. This is not a new plan, this is a continuance of a very old plan. The real question at hand, what Jesus is asking is: Do you love Me? More than Church traditions, more than your Church salary or housing? More than family or friends? If we truly love Jesus, God Almighty, we will seek to follow to the letter what He has spoken. We will search His Word diligently to be sure we are not mistaken and that we are prepared for the thief in the night!

THE FINAL STORY

OUTLINE OF END TIME FOR REFERENCE AND TEACHING:

I. Authority of Scripture
   a. John 12:48 – the word will judge us in the last day
   b. Revelation 20:12 – the books of people's lives and the Lamb's book
   c. 2 Peter 1:20 – Prophecy came as God moved on men
   d. 2 Thessalonians 2:10-13
   e. 2 Timothy 3:15 – 16 – All scripture is profitable
   f. John 5:39 – the scriptures testify of Jesus
   g. Matthew 5:17-20 – the law will be "fulfilled", not done away with
   h. Why study prophecy?
      i. Prophecy lays a foundation for the certainty of what we believe.
      ii. Concerning Jesus Christ, no man could have set up all the fulfillments to scripture that Jesus fulfilled
      iii. Prophecy establishes the certainty and absolute dependability of the word.
         1. All things come to past exactly as foretold
         2. All happened on the exact times that were given – like the feasts
      iv. Prophecy tells us:
         1. What to believe – the truth of scripture
         2. How to live it
         3. Where you are now in your personal walk with God and in God's time clock.
         4. Where you are going
         5. What manner of person God expects you to be
         6. Counsel to stand firm and not be shaken with His grace
         7. Assurance that God is in control and we can trust Him (#2, #6)

       i. Divisions of the Bible Chart – see pages 17 and 18 (#8)
II. The Spring Feasts of Israel – Prophecy laid out
   a. All the spring feasts were fulfilled on the exact month and day, setting a precedent.
   b. Feast of Passover = death
      i. Killed the Passover Lamb which must be without spot or blemish
      ii. Apply the blood of the Lamb on the doorposts of each Israelite door
      iii. Death angel will pass over when he sees the blood
      iv. Leviticus 23:5
      v. Exodus 12:21, 23
      vi. Christ became our Passover Lamb, our sinless sacrifice. Lamb slain from the foundation of the world. Our personal application is repentance.
      vii. 1 Corinthians 5:7
      viii. Isaiah 53:4-10
      ix. Colossians 3:2
   c. Feast of Unleavened Bread = Burial
      i. Actual feast celebrating Exodus. It was the second day after the Passover. They were commanded by God to clean out all leaven immediately after the Passover
      ii. Law of first mention: This establishes the meaning of a symbol.
         1. Luke 13:21
         2. Luke 12:1
         3. 1 Corinthians 5:6-8
         4. Matthew 16:12 (#6)
      iii. Leviticus 23:6
      iv. Exodus 12:19
      v. We are commanded by God to clean out all sin out of our lives
      vi. Acts 2:38 we are baptized in the name of Jesus for the remission of our sins

vii. 1 Peter 3:21 baptism saves us.
viii. 1 Corinthians 5:8
ix. Galatians 5:9
x. Romans 12:1-2
xi. 2 Corinthians 7:1
d. Feast of Firstfruits = Resurrection
i. It was the third day after the Passover. They kept this feast after entering into the Promised land, their inheritance
ii. Leviticus 23:10
iii. Exodus 12:15
iv. Jesus Christ rose from the dead and became the first to establish the new covenant – the Church.
v. 1 Corinthians 15:20-23
vi. Romans 11:16
e. Feast of Pentecost
i. Giving of the first fruits of the harvest. It marked a holy convocation and rest day. Pentecost occurred exactly 50 days after First Fruits and lasted a period of seven Sabbaths.
ii. Leviticus 23:15-21, Isaiah 28:11-12, Joel 2:28
iii. Jesus ascended and His disciples went to Jerusalem and waited for the promise of power. It had been 40 days since Feast of First Fruits when He resurrected. They had to wait 10 more days, fasting and praying, for the Day of Pentecost = 50 days.
iv. The number 50 is tied to the year of Jubilee when all slaves were freed and all inheritances were given back to their owners. Leviticus 23:9
v. This is the rest whereby the weary may rest and this is the refreshing. Isaiah 28:11-12, Acts 3:19
vi. John 3:5-8, Mark 16:16-20, Acts 19:1-6 (#2, #4, #5)
III. The Fall Feasts of Israel
a. "The Feast of Pentecost closed Israel's springtime festivals. After Pentecost, there were four long summer months, during which harvests were reaped before the next holy day which was the Feast of Trumpets. Leviticus 23:23-25 says, 'The Lord said to Moses, say to the

Israelites, on the first day of the seventh month, you are to have a day of rest, a sacred assembly, commemorated with trumpet blasts. Do no regular work, but present an offering made to the Lord by fire.' We are now faced with a surprising fact. The scriptures call for a sacred assembly commemorated with trumpet blasts. But instead, the Jewish calendar celebrates New Year's Day, Rosh Hashanah on that day! This is not just a question of which day is New Year's Day. It is evident that ancient Israel kept at least two calendars (the rabbis mentioned four). The civil calendar, which began in Nisan, and the religious calendar, which began in Tishri...One of the best known Jewish New Year's Day customs is the expression of the greeting, 'May you be inscribed for a good year!' This greeting is based on the belief that God judges the world on Rosh Hashanah. The Rabbis believe that the first of Tishri is the date of creation. The Mishnah (the written code of the oral law) speaks of it as a day of judgment when all men pass before the Creator as sheep are examined by the Shepherd. (4) (italics added).

    i. Krog commentary
    ii. important points:
       1. The harvests were reaped before the Feast of Trumpets blew. This anticipates a pre-Tribulation Rapture of Pentecost saints.
       2. It was an offering made to the Lord by fire. Matthew said, in his gospel (3:11), "...I indeed baptize you with water unto repentance. But He that cometh after me is mightier than I, whose shoes I am not worthy to bear: He shall baptize you with the Holy Ghost and with fire, whose fan is in His hand, and He will thoroughly purge His floor, and gather His wheat in to the garner but He will burn up the chaff with unquenchable fire.
       3. Acts 2:3-4 "And there appeared unto them cloven tongues like as of fire and it sat upon each of them. And they were all filled with the Holy Ghost and began to speak with other tongues as the Spirit gave them utterance." Romans 12:1-2
    b. Rosh Hashanah – Feast of Trumpets
       i. Begins on the first occurrence of the new moon. This is the only feast that has no set day. Mark 13:28 – 33, 1 Thessalonians

THE FINAL STORY

5:1 - 9
    ii. 1st Trumpet - Calling of the assembly and the 2nd trumpet - call for the journeying of the camps
    iii. Leviticus 23:23-24
    iv. Numbers 10:1-10, The two trumpets
    v. First trumpet blew in 1948 – Israel became a nation Numbers 10:7
    vi. Second trumpet will blow in the fall season (harvest) – the rapture of the Church Numbers 10:10
    vii. 1 Thessalonians 4:16-17
    viii. 1 Corinthians 15:51-53
    ix. Revelation 8:6 - NOT the Revelation trumpets. Those are judgment trumpets, not peace trumpets.
  c. Yom Kippur – Feast of Reconciliation
    i. Day of Atonement – Israel's national day of repentance
    ii. Jesus Christ will set foot on the Mt. of Olives with 10,000s of His saints and Israel will repent and declare Him their reigning Messiah. The waters of the Dead Sea will be healed. Jude 14, Zechariah 14:1-8, Ezekiel 47.
    iii. It is important to note that for 2000 years, Israel has not been able to keep this Day of Atonement. It requires a High Priest, a Temple and sacrifices.
    iv. Leviticus 23:27
    v. Daniel 9:24 – 26
    vi. Zechariah 12:9-10, 13:6-9, 14:12-21
    vii. Jesus Christ comes back with 10,000 of His saints and stand on the Mount of Olives. Revelation 16:16, Joel 3:14
    viii. Then all of Israel will be reconciled to Jesus as their reigning Messiah
  d. Feast of Tabernacles
    i. Leviticus 23:24
    ii. Zechariah 3:10
    iii. Year of Jubilee – time of rejoicing of the ingathering of God's people.

      iv. Millennium reign of the Messiah from Jerusalem

      v. Ends in the judgment of the Gentile nations that gathered to destroy Jerusalem

      vi. New heaven and new earth

      vii. Revelation 20:2 – 7

      viii.   Revelation 21:1 (#2, #5)

IV. Daniel

  a. 2:31 – 45 Image of Nebuchadnezzar

    i. Vision of one world dictator rule concerning the nation of Israel. Nebuchadnezzar's dream symbolizes world kingdoms that rule in succession. These stem from Babylon to the coming of Christ.

    ii. Two kingdoms of world dominance are not mentioned because they are already past. Those are Egypt and Assyria.

    iii. The next Babylon, indicated in Daniel 2:38.

    iv. The second kingdom is Media/Persia, mentioned in Daniel 5:30-31.

    v. The third kingdom is Greece, mentioned in Daniel 8:20-21.

    vi. The fourth kingdom is Rome, the two legs are the eastern and western division.

    vii. Daniel 9:26 mentions the prince that shall come, who was Titus, in A.D. 70. These kingdoms each grow weaker as represented by inferior metals. In the last days, the image is smote on the feet by a stone cut out of the mountain. That stone is Jesus Christ. Refer to Matthew 21:44. The kingdom following the stone is the millennial kingdom of Christ.

  b. Vision of the four beasts: Daniel had a vision 48 years after Nebuchadnezzar's dream. It was in the first year of Belshazzar's reign in B.C. 555. In this vision, Daniel stands on the shore of the Mediterranean, or Great Sea. Four kingdoms rise out of this sea in succession.

    i. The first was a Lion eagle's wings, Daniel 7:4. This is the sign of Babylon. The Lion is the king of beasts, and the eagle is the king of birds.

THE FINAL STORY

ii. The second beast was like a bear and had three ribs in his teeth, Daniel 7:5. The bear is the next strongest beast after the lion, but has none of the agility or majesty of the lion. It, however, conquers its prey with brute force. This is Media/Persia, which did not gain its victories by skill, but by use of vast numbers of troops. Xerxes campaigned against Greece, used 2,500,000 men. The three ribs in the mouth stand for the kingdoms of Lydia, Babylon and Egypt, which formed a triple alliance against Persia, but were all destroyed.

iii. The third beast was a leopard which had four wings of a fowl, and four heads, Daniel 7:6. The leopard is the most agile and graceful and its speed is assisted by wings. This is characteristic of the Greeks under Alexander the Great, who, in over 10 years, overthrew Persia and the whole civilized world. The four wings of the fowl indicate that it doesn't fly high, for lowland fighting.

iv. The four heads represent the four kingdoms that Greece was divided into at Alexander's death. These were Egypt, Syria, Thrace, and Macedonia. The fourth beast was unlike all others. Dreadful and terrible and strong exceedingly, and it had 10 horns, Daniel 7:7.

v. As Daniel considered the ten horns, he saw another little horn pluck up three of the first horns, Daniel 7:7-8. This is additional information that Nebuchadnezzar did not see, probably because it concerns God dealing with the Jewish people, in the latter days, Daniel 10:14. The little horn of the fourth beast troubled Daniel because it made war against "the saints of the Most High." These are Daniel's own God fearing Jews of the end time.

vi. The ten horns represent ten kings that shall arise. One king will subdue three of them, Daniel 10:8, 20.

c. Vision of the Ram and He-goat: While Daniel considered the vision of the ram, he saw a he-goat that had a "notable horn" between its eyes. It moved with anger against the ram, smote it with fury, broke its two horns and knocked it down. Then the he-goat grew great, but its great horn was broken off, and 4 horns came up in its place. Out of one of those sprang up a little horn that came against the "pleasant land" of Palestine, Daniel 8:5-9. The ram was Media/Persia with its two kings: Darius and his nephew, Cyrus. The he-goat was Greece, the great horn was Alexander the Great, and the four horns were the four generals that took over Alexander's kingdom.

    d. Why is all of this important? God revealed the future plan for reigning kingdoms of the world and their rulers. He foretold their deaths – both the nations and their rulers. These are told before the rulers were even born. Alexander the Great conquered all, but died suddenly at the age of 33 of swamp fever. This tells us that we are not left to chance. God has a plan and no one can do anything without the power given to them from up above (see John 19:10-11). This also sets a precedent. Things are fulfilled in chronological order. So one may discern where you are, and what events are to come in God's time line and in your life.

    e. The vision of the kings of the north and south – Daniel foresaw that the kingdom of Alexander would be divided into four kingdoms – Egypt, Syria, Thrace, Macedonia. Out of one of these will come the antichrist. Daniel was not told when this would happen.

        i. Daniel 11 – Tells exactly the history of the kings of Egypt and Syria for the next 350 years, which was future to Daniel. The wars of the kings of the north (Syria) and the kings of the south (Egypt) close with the reign of Antiochus Epiphanes – 164 B.C. (Refer to the Book of Maccabees) Verses 32-35 cover the whole period of time from 164 B.C. to the time of the end.

        ii. Chapter 11:36 mentions a willful king (the antichrist) and from that verse to the end of Daniel, we have an account of what will occur to Daniel's people (the Jews) in the latter days.

    f. Daniel's 70 weeks – in Daniel 9:24, we are told "seventy weeks are determined on thy people and on the holy city" to:
        i. Finish transgression
        ii. To make an end of sins
        iii. To make reconciliation for iniquity
        iv. To bring in everlasting righteousness
        v. To seal up the prophecy and the vision
        vi. To anoint the most holy

g. Daniel received this information in 538 B.C., the same year was the first year of Darius the Mede that brought the fall of Babylon. Daniel had been studying Jeremiah and learned that 70 years of captivity for his people would soon end, Jeremiah 25:11. Their captivity began in 606 B.C. and 68 years had elapsed. This caused Daniel to fast and pray about their release.

    i. Gabriel is sent to Daniel to give him revelation. The 70 weeks mentioned have nothing to do with the Gentiles or the gentile Church. The 70 weeks, or 490 years, only covers the time period when the Jews are, by God's permission, dwelling in their own land. This does not include the dispersion among the nations.

    ii. The expression "70 weeks" should read 70 sevens, because the Hebrew word "Heptad" means 7. Whether that is 7 days, weeks, or years, must be determined by the context. The 70 weeks are divided into 3 periods.

    1. 7 weeks and 62 weeks = 69 weeks from the "going forth of the commandment to restore and build Jerusalem unto Messiah the Prince".

    a. The date of this commandment is found in Nehemiah 2:1 – month of Nissan in the 20th year of Artaxerxes the king which was the 14th day of March, 445 B.C. The day when Jesus rode into Jerusalem as Messiah the Prince was Palm Sunday – April 2, 30 A.D. Luke 19:37-40, fulfilling that prophecy almost to the day. With proof like this, how did they miss the Messiah???

    b. We read that Messiah was to be cut off, but not for Himself. We then read a prince that shall come will destroy the city and the sanctuary (Temple). This was fulfilled in A.D. 70 by Titus. Matthew 24:2.

    c. The prophecy of the 70 weeks stopped, or was put on hold at the 69th week when Messiah was cut off. We have had 2000 years of the Church age that Daniel did not see, because the prophecy only concerned his people. So there is yet to be fulfilled a "one week" or 7 year period to be accomplished on the Jewish nation.

    2. 1 week – Gentile rule of the world will come to an end

during this last week. This is important to understand to comprehend the book of Revelation. The Church is not mentioned after chapter 5 in Revelation, so most of the book of Revelation deals with the Jews.

    3. In Luke 21:24, Jesus says that Jerusalem will be trodden down of the Gentiles until the "times of the Gentiles" be fulfilled. Romans 11:25 (#2, #3, #6, #9, #10)

V. Revelation

    a. Chapter 1:8 – Jesus says He is "the beginning and the ending, which was, which is and is to come, the Almighty"

    b. Chapters 2 and 3 – written to the Gentile Church. The word "Church" is not mentioned after chapter 3.

    c. Chapter 4 – shows one throne in heaven and one on the throne. He is called, in verse 8, "the Lord God Almighty, which was, which is, and is to come." And in verse 5 He is revealed as the Lion of the Tribe of Judah, the root of David.

    d. Chapter 6 and after – He that is on the throne is the Lamb. The Lamb breaks seals, trumpets, vials – the wrath of God. This begins the last 7 year period, or Daniel's 70th week which is upon the Jewish people only. This excludes Gentile Church which was established at the day of Pentecost and has been growing for 2000 years.

    e. Romans 11:25 full number of the Gentiles

    f. The Bible states the Church is not subject to the wrath of God

        i. In chapter 5, the four and twenty elders are in heaven.

        ii. Revelation 6, the seals contain the wrath of God.

        iii. Revelation 7 mentions the tribes of the children of Israel (still on the earth).

        iv. 1 Thessalonians 1:10

        v. 1 Thessalonians 5:9

    g. Gentile Church must be removed first because we have authority over devils and the antichrist cannot work while the Church of Jesus Christ is in this world.

        i. 2 Thessalonians 2:3 – 14

        ii. Mark 3:15, 6:7, 16:17

        iii. Matthew 10:1, 8

THE FINAL STORY

      iv. 1 John 4:4
      v. Luke 9:1; 10:19
   h. Revelation Judgments
      i. Seals, trumpets and vials
         1. Seal – holds that judgment until it is time.
         2. Trumpet – signals that the Seal has been opened
         3. Vial – signals that the judgment is being "poured out" on the earth.
      ii. Chapter 6 – all of the first 4 horsemen are the antichrist switching horses
         1. White – peace plan
         2. Red – war
         3. Black – has balances which finance the war. Also famine.
         4. Pale – death and disease.
      iii. Chapter 7 – 144,000 are all Jews. This is Daniel's 70th week to end all Gentile rule on the earth, to reveal to the Jews their Messiah and to usher in the millennial reign. Romans 11:25 blindness in part has happened to Israel until the full number of Gentiles be come in. (#1, #2, #6, #7, #9, #10)

VI. Mystery Babylon
   a. Revelation 17 hold a key to understanding much of the book of Revelation
      i. 17:1 there is a person called "the Great Whore". In 17:2 the book tells us that kings of the earth have committed fornication with her and have become drunk with the wine of her fornication.
      ii. 17:3 the Whore is called a woman who is full of the names of blasphemy. She sits on the Beast (the governmental system) which has 7 heads and 10 horns.
      iii. 17:4 gives me a clue. The woman is clothed in purple and scarlet and is ornamented with gold and precious stones. I am further told she has a golden cup in her hand full of abominations and fornications.
      iv. 17:5 on her forehead is a name – Mystery Babylon the

Great, the mother of harlots and abominations on the earth.

    v. 17:6 She is drunk with the blood of the saints and martyrs of Jesus.

    vi. 17:7 the angel is about to give the understanding of the Mystery (former verses).

    vii. 17:8 the Beast was and is not and yet is. This is speaking of the Roman Empire.

    viii. 17:9 the mind which has wisdom will understand the 7 heads are 7 mountains on which the Whore sits. This is a geographic location.

    ix. 17:10 There are seven kings, 5 are fallen at the time of John the Revelator, one is, and one is yet to come. These correspond to Egypt, Assyria, Babylon, Medio/Persia, and Greece. These are the 5 which are fallen. The one that is, is Rome ruled by Caesars. The one which is to come is the 10 kingdom alliance of the antichrist.

    x. 17:11 the Beast is of those 7. The Beast is one world dictator rule concerning the people of God (Israel).

    xi. 17:12 the 10 horns are 10 kings. Most likely the ECM (European Common Market)

    xii. 17:13 These have one mind which means they are in unity. In 1993 they referred to themselves as "The Country". Their one currency is the Euro. Watch this group.

    xiii. 17:14 these shall make war with the Lamb. The Lord of lords and King of kings shall overcome them and it mentions a group – "they that are with Him (already) are called, chosen and faithful." Let's pause here and talk about this. There is only one city that sets on 7 hills. It is Rome. Later on in this chapter, this will be confirmed as Papal Rome. N where in these two chapters is this woman referred to as "the Church." That term was last used in Revelation chapter 3. So the question is, who are these who are with Him?

    xiv. 17:15 The woman (the whore) is over peoples, multitudes, nations, and tongues. This means she is everywhere.

    xv. 17:16 the political Beast will hate the woman and destroy her.

THE FINAL STORY

xvi. 17:17 God has put in their hearts to hate her. Sounds like a severe judgment to me.

xvii. 17:18 The woman is that great city that reigns over the kings of the earth. Here is a piece of wisdom, the Pope and Cardinals crowned and excommunicated kings. We must ask ourselves why God called her "Mystery Babylon?" Obviously He is not talking about the literal city of Babylon, but its attitude and philosophy. To understand Babylon, we must look at the scriptures where this is first mentioned.

1. Genesis 9:1, 7 we find God gives a command to be fruitful, multiply and replenish the earth.

2. When we come to Genesis 11:4, we find the people in rebellion, deciding to build a city and tower dedicated to the heavens and make themselves a name and do not be scattered throughout the earth.

3. 11:6 the Lord confuses their language to separate them. We find the establishment of the tower of Babel and its city as an act of rebellion against God. This plays out in history and archeology, the beginning of multiple gods to be worshipped began in Babylon. Idolatry also began in Babylon. Nimrod and his wife, Semiramis, and her son, Tammuz, were worshipped as gods. Her name in Egypt is Isis, and Osiris. The Assyrians called her Ishtar. The Phoenicians called her Astarte and her son, Baal. (#7) Therefore, we find the attitude of Babylon apostasy from the truth of God, and rebellion to God's commands. Babylon also worshipped idols, zodiac, spiritism, etc. Nimrod desired to be a one world dominate leader and to ensnare the people. These attitudes, therefore, we might expect to find in the woman whom God calls a harlot and Mystery Babylon. The whoredoms and fornications mentioned in Revelation 17 are doctrinal errors.

b. Revelation 18

i. 18:2 an angel comes down and declares that Rome is fallen, is the habitation of devils and hold of every foul spirit and the cage of every unclean and hateful bird. Strong language. Do you suppose God wants us to pay attention to her description?

ii. 18:3 The wrath of her fornication and kings of the earth have committed fornication with her and the merchants of the earth are made rich by her delicacies. This speaks of partaking of her doctrines and her lavish spending on garments, jewels, and buildings.

iii. 18:4 issues an eternal warning: I heard a voice from heaven saying come out of her my people that you be not partakers of her sins and that you receive not of her plagues. It would behoove us to learn what her doctrines are and search the scriptures whether the apostles of Jesus Christ taught such things.

iv. 18:16, 17 She is destroyed in one hour.

v. 18:20 The Apostles and Prophets in heaven rejoice over her destruction.

vi. This whore had children. The word "protestant" means to protest. The word "reformation" means to reform. What were they protesting and what were they reforming? All of the reformers had Roman Catholic roots, and were discovering and declaring abuses and false doctrines. Each of the reformers carried a valid point, but usually had to run and hide for their lives. Therefore, they did not have enough means to discover everything, and their followers became movements. Since we are commanded to come out of her, we should research what teachings she gives that so angered the Lord. 1 Timothy 4:1-5. Anyone wanting a list of Catholic doctrines contrary to the word of God, please ask Dennis Krog. (#1, #2, #6, #7, #9, #10)

 1. Seven Ecumenical Councils
 2. School of the Scriptures – Catholic doctrines

VII. Millennial Reign of Jesus Christ
 a. Peace on earth, Isaiah 2:4, 9:6-7, Revelation 2:26-27
 b. Sickness and disease gone Isaiah 65:19-20, 35:5-6
 c. Men will live long lives Isaiah 65:22
 d. Thorns and thistles gone Isaiah 11:9, 65:23, 35:1, 7, Zechariah 8:12
 e. Viciousness gone from animals Isaiah 11:6-9
 f. All nations will worship at Jerusalem Zechariah 14:9, 16-19, Isaiah 11:9

    g. Saints reign with Christ 1 Corinthians 6:2-3, Revelation 1:5-6, 5:8-10, 20:6, 1 Corinthians 15:52-54, 1 Thessalonians 4:17

    h. satan loosed after 1000 years. Gathers the armies of Gog and Magog to battle against God Revelation 20:7-9

    i. This period ends in judgment

VIII. White Throne judgment

    a. satan cast into the Lake of Fire Revelation 20:10

    b. Second resurrection of the unjust. Revelation 20:11-13

    c. Men will be judged Romans 2:12-16, Proverbs 1:24-31, Matthew 7:21-23

    d. Those names not in the Book of Life, are cast into the Lake of Fire Revelation 20:15

    e. The devil and his angels Matthew 25:41, slothful servants, Matthew 25:26-30, backsliders Hebrews 10:29, the ungodly 2 Peter 3:7, those that did not love and buy the truth 2 Thessalonians 2:8-10, those that did not obey the gospel 2 Thessalonians 1:8, all will be cast into the Lake of Fire.

    f. New heaven and new earth Isaiah 51:6, 65:17, 2 Peter 3:7-13

    g. New Jerusalem John 14:2-3, Revelation 21, 22:1-5

    h. He is coming quickly Revelation 22:7, 12-14, 17-20

BIBLIOGRAPHY

Barker, K. L., Kohlenberger, J. R. III (1994) The Expositor's Bible Comentary: Abridged Edition. New Testament. Zondervan. Michigan: Grand Rapids.

Bible (1931) Dickson New Analytical Study Bible, King James Version. World Bible Publishers, Michigan: Grand Rapids.

Bicklein, R. N. (1985) Prophetic Time Periods. Bookworld Publishing Company, Inc. Florida, Orlando.

Dugas, P. D. ((1983) The Feasts of Jehovah in Prophecy. Apostolic Book Publishers OR: Portland.

Fuchs, D. (1985) Israel's Holy Days: In Type and Prophecy. Loizeaux Brothers, New Jersey: Neptune.

Krog, D. Personal insights and commentary.

McDonald, J. (1983) The Plan for the Planet. The Plan for the Planet Publications, Texas: Houston.

Search for Truth #1 (1965) 10 Lesson Bible Study, Word Aflame Press. Missouri: Hazelwood.

Stoneking, L. School of Scriptures – Tabernacle of Joy. Syllabus from Apostolic Bible Institute, St. Paul, MN. Retrieved, 2011 by Linda Krog. Website: www.apostolichub.com.

Strong, J. (1990) Strong's Exhaustive Concordance of the Bible. Nashville, TN: Thomas Nelson.

Thayer, T.A. (2000) Thayer's Greek-English Lexicon of the New Testament. Peabody, MA: Hendrickson Publishers, Inc.

Unger, M.F. (1957) The New Unger's Bible Dictionary. Chicago: Moody Press.

Urshan, J. (1987-1991) Preaching notes. Bethel Pentecostal Church, St. Peters, MO.

ADDITIONAL END TIME SCRIPTURES

(not an exhaustive list):
Amos 9:8-15
Isaiah 34:1-17
Isaiah 66:15-24
Ezekiel 9:4-7, 11:17-21, 46 all, 47 all, 48 all
Hosea 13:14-16, 14:1-9
Joel 2:28-32
Micah 5:1-4
Zephaniah 3:11-20
Haggai 2:6-9, 21-23
Zechariah all
Malachi 3:1, 16-18, 4:1-6
Psalms 50:1-6, 86:9, 96:10-13, 97:1-6, 98:9, 110:1-7 (just a few)
Matthew 22:7-14
Matthew 24 all
1 Thessalonians 5:1-11
2 Thessalonians 1:6-12, 2:1-15
2 Timothy 3:1-7
Hebrews 12:22-29
James 5:7-12
1 Peter 4:3-8, 17-19
2 Peter 3:1-18
Jude 14-16

A study of the Mosaic Law is excluded. However, there are several references there also.

DENNIS & LINDA KROG

DIVISIONS OF THE BOOKS OF THE BIBLE:

OLD TESTAMENT
Law of Moses
Genesis
Exodus
Leviticus
Numbers
Deuteronomy
Historical Books
Joshua
Judges
Ruth
1 Samuel
2 Samuel
1 Kings
2 Kings
1 Chronicles
2 Chronicles
Ezra
Nehemiah
Esther
Poetry
Job
Psalms
Proverbs
Ecclesiastes
Songs of Solomon
Prophecy
Major Prophets
Isaiah
Jeremiah
Lamentations
Ezekiel

Minor Prophets
Daniel
Hosea
Joel
Amos
Obadiah
Jonah
Micah
Nahum
Habakkuk
Zephaniah
Haggai
Zechariah
Malachi

NEW TESTAMENT
Gospels
Matthew
Mark
Luke
John
Birth of the Church
Acts
Pauline Epistles
Romans
1 Corinthians
2 Corinthians
Galatians
Ephesians
Philippians
Colossians
1 Thessalonians

2 Thessalonians
1 Timothy
2 Timothy
Titus
Philemon
General Epistles
Hebrews
James
1 Peter
2 Peter
1 John
2 John
3 John
Jude
Prophecy
Revelation

THE FINAL STORY

Made in the USA
Columbia, SC
25 November 2018